Benefits of FASTING

JOHN K. WILLIAM

Benefits of Fasting

ISBN: 978-9966-8219-5-9

Printed in the Republic of Kenya.

Published by:

Brook Publishers Limited
P.O. Box 14185-20100, Nakuru.
Tel. +254 722 344 360 / 0799 573 310
Email: brookpublishers@gmail.com

CONTENTS

ACKNOWLEDGMENT

First and foremost, I thank the Almighty God for giving me the grace to serve Him in my generation. Had He not provoked me to serve Him, I would not be where I am today. Glory be to His name.

Secondly, to my wife and co-worker, Rev. Naomi Kimani for her moral and spiritual support in my life and ministry. I am indebted for your valuable contributions and prayers.

To the Kingdom Seekers Fellowship Family and MBCI Partners; your partnership in my ministry is very encouraging. May the Lord bless you abundantly.

Finally, I am grateful to our Publishing Team, for your work in professionally preparing this book for publishing. This book would not have been out without your untiring efforts. God bless you.

DEDICATION

I dedicate this book to all believers who desire to experience the many benefits that accompany prayer and fasting. Your commitment to seeking God in this way will unlock both spiritual and material blessings that will change your life.

PREFACE

Fasting is one of the spiritual disciplines that are taught in the Bible. The Word of God gives many straightforward instructions and examples of fasting and records what it can help mankind to achieve. However, not many believers are aware that they can fast effectively and in so doing obtain many profitable things from it. I believe that the main reason for this is ignorance of the spiritual and physical benefits it avails to those who practice it.

One of the reasons why many Christians do not fast often is that they focus more on what they miss while fasting instead of what they are bound to receive. Believers should understand that the food they forgo when they fast cannot be compared to the benefits that result from fasting.

Fasting is abstaining from food and drink for the purpose of seeking God. It consists of a time of breaking the routine so that one can spend quality time with God. The length of time and the intensity with which one fasts depend on the seriousness of the matter they are dealing with and the number of benefits they are seeking to obtain.

The Bible teaches four types of fasting. The first is an absolute fast in which one neither eats nor drinks anything for three days (Esther 4:16 and Acts 9:9). Some people like Moses took forty days of absolute fasting. One should not exceed three days without food and drink unless they have heard clearly from God. The second is a normal fast in which one does not eat anything but drinks water (Matthew 4:2). The third is a partial fast in which one abstains from certain choice types of foods for a certain period (Daniel 10:2-3). The fourth is the fasted life. This happens when a believer takes an extended period of fasting for many days and only eats when he or she feels weak and in need of strength. Any of these types of fasting is acceptable to God provided one does it with the right motive and by faith.

All followers of Jesus should know that what they can get from God through fasting is more valuable than what one may lose. It is true that food is one of the many awesome blessings God provides to humanity for enjoyment (1 Timothy

6:17). However, we must not forget that the word of God also says that man does not live by bread alone but by every word that proceeds from the mouth of God (Matthew 4:4). This makes it necessary for every man and woman who desires to truly glorify God to learn to sacrifice their appetite for food regularly. That way, they can allow the Lord to intervene in their lives in a way that is only possible through His mighty supernatural power. Fasting is a divinely ordained discipline for reinforcing prayer which is the heartbeat of the life of a Christian.

There are many tragic examples in the Bible of people whose lives would have been different from what they were if they took the call to fast and pray seriously. Their failure to subject their desire for food to the plan and will of God cost them their lives and destinies. Food is a good slave but a terrible master and we should not allow it to master us. This is why every child of God needs to crucify their appetite and in that way get hold of the many benefits and blessings that God only gives to those that obey His call to fast.

It is the duty of every child of God to fast so that they can take possession of their inheritance in God. Fasting is literally hungering and thirsting for the righteousness of God (Matthew 5:6) and He is faithful to reward all those who seek Him diligently.

It is my hope and prayer that through the contents in this book, you will learn the many benefits that come through fasting. I also pray that reading this book will release the grace you need in your life so that you can fast and pray more than you have ever done in your life.

Chapter 1

THE PRESENCE OF GOD

Many godly people desire to enjoy the presence of God wherever they are. This is a good desire because His presence brings peace, joy, satisfaction, assurance and many other blessings. However, like every other thing of great value, the presence of God does not come free of charge. The greatest key to the presence of God is prayer that is reinforced by fasting.

The willingness by man to go without food that is so crucial to his sustenance in the physical realm touches the heart of God and it acts as a magnet for Him to manifest His presence.

The Bible teaches this through the example of the Lord Jesus Christ. He fasted for forty days and forty nights at the beginning of His earthly ministry. It records that Jesus was full of the Holy Spirit as He headed into the wilderness for a time of seeking God. After forty days and nights of fasting, He returned to Galilee in the power of the Holy Spirit.

> *Jesus, full of the Holy Spirit, returned from the Jordan and was led by the Spirit in the desert... Jesus returned to Galilee in the power of the Spirit, and news about him spread through the whole countryside.* - Luke 4:1, 14

The key that moved Him from being FULL of the Spirit to returning IN the power of the Spirit was fasting. As He went without food, His spirit was configured and empowered by the Father to be a perfect dwelling place from where the Spirit could manifest His power and glory. News about Him spread like wild fire once He was full of God's presence.

Prince (1973) makes the following observations concerning the fasting of Jesus Christ:

> It would appear that the potential of the Holy Spirit's power, which Jesus received at the time of His baptism in Jordan, only came forth into full manifestation after He had completed His fast. Fasting was the final phase of preparation through which He had to pass, before entering into His public ministry.

The same privilege that Jesus had is available to all believers today if they will devote themselves to seeking God with fasting.

During the course of His teachings to His disciples, Jesus told them that the discipline of fasting would be the key to unlocking His presence once He was no longer with them physically. His presence in the flesh with His followers guaranteed them His help and the comfort that only He has the power to offer at any time. However, once He left, fasting would be the password to draw Him near to them.

Fasting was recognised as a valid spiritual exercise and the followers of John the Baptist and the Pharisees used to engage in it as well. For a short while in the time Jesus was physically with them, Jesus exempted His disciples from it. He however made it clear to them that they too, would need to practice it once He was departed from their midst.

> *They said to him, "John's disciples often fast and pray, and so do the disciples of the Pharisees, but yours go on eating and drinking." Jesus answered, "Can you make the guests of the bridegroom fast while he is with them? But the time will come when the bridegroom will be taken from them; in those days they will fast."* - Luke 5:33-34

The truth in this Scripture implies that believers cannot be effective in their faith, calling, ministries and lives as a whole without relying on the presence of God. God designed man to be truly fruitful only in His presence and with His help. This is why He created a special environment that was

believers cannot be effective in their faith, calling, ministries and lives as a whole without relying on the presence of God

saturated with His presence when He created man to dwell there. The name of that place was the Garden of Eden.

Now the LORD God had planted a garden in the east, in Eden; and there he put the man he had formed. - Genesis 2:8

This garden was not just a physical place but it carried with it a special spiritual atmosphere that was conducive for both God and man. Fasting brings the presence of God to us as it was in the Garden of Eden. This has been made possible by the atoning sacrifice of Jesus Christ who opened the way for us to have direct and unlimited access to the throne of God. The Bible invites us to draw near the throne of grace with confidence so that we can receive mercy and grace to help us whenever we are in need.

> *Let us then approach the throne of grace with confidence, so that we may receive mercy and find grace to help us in our time of need. - Hebrews 4:16*

The name of the garden bears a lot of significance. Eden is Hebrew word that means five things, namely:

1. A spot
2. A moment
3. An open door
4. Presence
5. Access

It was an environment that was conducive for man to carry out the mandate God had given Him. It was a location that had unlimited favour from God and He found great delight in it. It was also a place where each moment of day and night was characterised by the tangible presence of God because it was free from sin, corruption and uncleanness which are against His holy nature. The Garden of Eden was a place that had an open door into the heavenly realm from where God would exercise authority over the rest of the earth.

The Garden of Eden was a place that had an open door into the heavenly realm from where God would exercise authority over the rest of the earth

His presence was unlimited and man's access to the supernatural was secure. It gave the Lord great delight to regularly visit Adam and Eve in that holy environment. The Bible says that God would come and walk in Garden in the cool of the day.

> *Then the man and his wife heard the sound of the LORD God as he was walking in the garden in the cool of the day, and they hid from the LORD God among the trees of the garden.* - Genesis 3:8

God's plan in creating man was that He would exercise dominion and authority over the creation using the delegated power He had given him. He wanted to have man fill the whole earth with His presence so that the earth would reflect the glory of heaven with man as the chief agent of that work.

> *Then God said, "Let us make man in our image, in our likeness, and let them rule over the fish of the sea and the birds of the air, over the livestock, over all the earth, and over all the creatures that move along the ground."* - Genesis 1:26

The plan of God is that His will shall be done on the earth as it is in heaven. This is why Jesus taught His disciples to pray that the will of the Father will be done here as it is in heaven (Matthew 6:10).

The exercise of the power and dominion God gave man was (and still is) only possible through divine enablement. This help is only accessible in the presence of God from where every good and perfect gift comes (James 1:17). Man was not meant to be independent of God because he was a steward over God's creation. This has not changed today because we belong to God and all we have is from Him.

Man's rebellion caused him to be banished from the Garden of God's presence because God required obedience from him as a condition of remaining in that environment. Man's fall into sin was thus a catastrophic event that made God drive him away from His presence and put the Garden under tight security lest man sneaks in.

> *So the LORD God banished him from the Garden of Eden to work the ground from which he had been taken. After he drove the man out, he placed on the east side of the Garden of Eden cherubim and a flaming sword flashing back*

> *and forth to guard the way to the tree of life.* - Genesis 3:23-24

All human beings after Adam are born in an environment that is away from the presence of God. After being reconciled to God after salvation, it becomes necessary to seek God with fasting because His presence in our lives is not automatic as it was in Eden.

Just as the presence of God in the Garden of Eden was meant to help man to be productive, the presence of God helps believers to manifest the fullness of what God has placed in them. God has graciously endued every believer potential, gifts, talents and abilities which He desires man to use in a profitable way to glorify Him and serve others. These find their best expression and manifestation in God's presence. Franklin (2008) says that "God wants to pour out supernatural blessings in our lives, but they will never be realized if we are not willing to seek Him in fasting and prayer." Believers need to fast to appropriate this empowering presence.

The Bible demonstrates this truth using the example of Aaron. When the Israelites grumbled constantly against the Levitical priesthood, God commanded them to put twelve staffs, one representing each tribe of Israel, before His presence so that He could settle the dispute. As He had promised, the rod of the man He had chosen would bud and bear fruit. That settled the debate once for all.

> *The next day Moses entered the Tent of the Testimony and saw that Aaron's staff, which represented the house of Levi, had not only sprouted but had budded, blossomed and produced almonds.* - Numbers 17:8

Believers who take time to fast and seek God receive a spiritual mark of productivity that sets them apart from all other people. Many of the disputes we witness today would be settled for good if disciples spent quality time with God in fasting.

Believers who take time to fast and seek God receive a spiritual mark of productivity that sets them apart from all other people

God is a prudent and committed entrepreneur. He makes a point of taking personalised care for

His people by appearing in person to do His duties the same way a farmer attends to his crops. In John 15:1, Jesus describes the Father as the gardener. No serious gardener can take care of his orchard without physically appearing in it to prune, tend and water his plants so that they can bear much fruit. Fasting helps us to draw near to God which activates His promise to us that those who move close to Him are going to have more of Him.

> *Come near to God and he will come near to you. Wash your hands, you sinners, and purify your hearts, you double-minded.* - James 4:8

Another important thing to note is that in the presence of God there is productivity. God is highly glorified when His people bear much fruit. Fasting acts as an outward sign that one is actually chosen of God and is ready to forfeit all manner of worldly comforts to bear spiritual fruit that has lasting value.

> *You did not choose me, but I chose you and appointed you to go and bear fruit - fruit that will last. Then the Father will give you whatever you ask in my name.* - John 15:16

Only the believers who submit to the discipline

of the Father through allowing Him to prune them through fasting can bear fruit. Fasting is deliberately yielding authority over your body and giving it to God to refine it so that you can bear spiritual fruit. It is pursuing spiritual benefits at the expense of the few physical benefits one may derive from continuously taking nourishment for their body.

When Christians fast and experience the presence of God, it comes with a purifying effect because it exposes sin and all unfruitful works. This helps them to deal with them so that they pursue sanctification and glorify God.

> *Everyone who has this hope in him purifies himself, just as he is pure. But you know that he appeared so that he might take away our sins. And in him is no sin.* - 1 John 3:3, 5

One of the biggest problems of our day is stress and depression. Many people have sunk into the doldrums of despair because of the many challenges that abound in the world. When believers fast to seek the presence of the Lord, they receive His supernatural joy that not only comforts them but also empowers them to face challenges with confidence.

> *You have made known to me the path of life; you will fill me with joy in your presence, with eternal pleasures at your right hand.* - Psalm 16:11

When believers fast to pursue the presence of God, the Lord gives them comfort and assurance. Apostle Paul admonished the saints in Philippi to pray about everything and worry about nothing. He told them that such a lifestyle would avail to them the peace of God that transcends all human understanding (Philippians 4:7). If prayer alone can achieve such a supernatural result, reinforcing it with fasting can help us achieve far much more.

Fasting also helps us to appropriate the presence of God which opens doors that were previously closed. The Lord holds in His hand the key of David that opens closed doors in a manner that no man can shut. This is especially true of those who keep His word (which includes practicing the discipline of fasting) and refuse to deny His name.

> *"To the angel of the church in Philadelphia write: These are the words of him who is holy and true, who holds the key of David. What he opens no one can shut, and what he shuts no one can open. I know your deeds. See, I have placed before you an open door that no one can shut. I know that you have little strength, yet you have kept my word and have not denied my name.* - Revelation 3:7-8

Fasting also helps one to know the Lord better and in a deeper way. God is in dimensions and we need to seek more of His heights. We will experience more of His glory if we will be willing to forfeit food for Him.

> *Not that I have already obtained all this, or have already been made perfect, but I press on to take hold of that for which Christ Jesus took hold of me. Brothers, I do not consider myself yet to have taken hold of it. But one thing I do: Forgetting what is behind and straining toward what is ahead.* - Philippians 3:12-13

Another benefit believers receive from the presence of God is that it gives them life. The presence of God gives life. The Lord invites all those who believe in Him to seek Him and live

(Amos 5:14). The life He offers is abundant and incomparable to any other thing.

> *The thief comes only to steal and kill and destroy; I have come that they may have life, and have it to the full.* - John 10:10

The presence of God creates an enabling environment for the purposes and plans of God to be carried to completion. This agrees with a famous quote by Saint Augustine in which he said: Without God, man cannot, and without man, God will not. The Lord has chosen to bear fruit on the earth through His followers who He has made the branches in the tree that He is - the vine.

The presence of God creates an enabling environment for the purposes and plans of God to be carried to completion

> *"I am the true vine, and my Father is the gardener. He cuts off every branch in me that bears no fruit, while every branch that does bear fruit he prunes so that it will be even more fruitful.* - John 15:1-2

Every child of God should value the presence

of God and be willing to make all the sacrifices necessary to enjoy -including fasting. The presence of God is so important because we are nothing and can do nothing without it (John 15:4). Moses recognised this and asked the Lord not to send him and the children of Israel away without His Presence.

> *The LORD replied, "My Presence will go with you, and I will give you rest." Then Moses said to him, "If your Presence does not go with us, do not send us up from here.* - Exodus 33:14-15

All believers should have such a desire as Moses had because when the Lord avails His presence in our lives, He gives us rest and divine comfort that we cannot get anywhere else. In fact, every Christian who sets aside times to fast and pray should make a point of asking God to manifest His presence in his or her life through the power of the Holy Spirit.

When believers fast, they enjoy the presence of the God through His Holy Spirit. His coming gives liberty to those who are enslaved and bound by forces of darkness that try to hinder them from seeing Him in His glory.

> *Now the Lord is the Spirit, and where the Spirit of the Lord is, there is freedom.* - 2 Corinthians 3:17

All followers of Jesus should take comfort in the truth that Jesus has promised to be present with them till the end of the age (Matthew 28:20). Like all the other promises of God in His word, this is a sure commitment and we would do well to receive and activate it by faith and with fasting.

Chapter 2

SECURING OUR DESTINIES

The secular world defines destiny as the events that will necessarily happen to a person or thing in the future. That is a good definition but it only captures a small part of what destiny is. Destiny may be defined as the sum total of what God created you to be in this life and in eternity. It brings together every area of life – the intellectual, social, financial, marital, spiritual as well as eternal life. The important thing we all need to know is that although it is the will of God, destiny cannot be fulfilled without man's involvement. Man is not meant to be a passive observer as his life takes the journey of destiny but should be at the driver's seat of his life.

The word of God teaches that God has a good plan and purpose for each human being. He desires to see it fulfilled because He wants to see a good end for all His people. He extends His benevolence to us by making all the plans necessary to make us successful.

Man is not meant to be a passive observer as his life takes the journey of destiny but should be at the driver's seat of his life

For I know the plans I have for you," declares the LORD, "plans to prosper you and not to harm you, plans to give you hope and a future.
- Jeremiah 29:11

Fasting helps us to activate the purpose of God in our lives. All the purposes of God are first and foremost a spiritual reality before they manifest in the physical realm. Therefore, man needs to connect with God in the Spirit realm to activate his destiny. Just as it is impossible to enjoy the light from a bulb without first switching it on, we cannot live in the fullness of our destiny without connecting with the God who designed it for us.

Destiny has many enemies. Some of them are spiritual while others are physical. Among the physical adversaries of purpose, the stomach ranks very high in the list. Many millions of people have lost or aborted their destinies because of their inability to suppress their appetite for food.

Consider the example of Esau. He was the firstborn son of Isaac, the son of Abraham. He had a twin brother by the name Jacob. As a firstborn, Esau had the right to inherit twice as much as his younger brother as that was the custom of his people. This right could be traded if the person who held it felt they wanted to sell it for something they considered more valuable than it. Jacob took advantage of a moment of weakness

Just as it is impossible to enjoy the light from a bulb without first switching it on, we cannot live in the fullness of our destiny without connecting with the God who designed it for us

in Esau's character and asked him to sell him the birthright.

> *Once when Jacob was cooking some stew, Esau came in from the open country, famished. He said to Jacob, "Quick, let me have some of that red stew! I'm famished!" (That is why he was also called Edom.) Jacob replied, "First sell me your birthright." "Look, I am about to die," Esau said. "What good is the birthright to me?" But Jacob said, "Swear to me first." So he swore an oath to him, selling his birthright to Jacob. Then Jacob gave Esau some bread and some lentil stew. He ate and drank, and then got up and left. So Esau despised his birthright.* - Genesis 25:29-34

At this point, Esau's rights as a firstborn did not have so much physical significance because his father was still alive. Its full benefits would be his as soon as his father was dead because that would be the time for him to receive his inheritance. Instead of holding firm to the promise for the future, Esau deliberately chose to indulge in his fleshly desires of the moment and ended up missing his inheritance. His many tears to recover what the blessing had lost were in vain (Hebrews

12:17). He allowed his appetite for food to reign supreme over all spiritual realities in his life. He thus missed what really mattered – his destiny.

Writing about fasting and the role it plays in activating the purposes of God in a person's life, Franklin (2008) says that believers need to understand that the Bible is a book that is full of promises "but some of them will never be realised as long as King Stomach rules your appetite and controls your life."

As Franklin indicates, the stomach is a terrible master and has the potential of taking the path of a person's life down the road to destruction. That is why it is necessary for all people who desire to fulfill the purposes of God to dethrone it by regular fasting. Fasting is without a doubt an inconvenient and troublesome discipline but the pain and loss of your destiny is far worse than the hunger

the Bible is a book that is full of promises "but some of them will never be realised as long as King Stomach rules your appetite and controls your life

pangs you might have to endure for a few hours or days while you are at it. It requires a generous amount of effort to remove this merciless dictator from the thrones of our hearts and enthrone the will of God in our lives. However, it is all worth the effort.

Esau's sin not only cost him dearly but it was also a constant thorn in the flesh of his descendants, the Edomites. They later became an accursed people and enemies of God's people because they were mean towards Israel (Numbers 20:18). They took this evil streak from their ancestor who was also called Edom. Their actions attracted God's wrath because they were as godless as their forefather.

In his greed, lack of self-control and disregard of the great value of his birthright, Esau sold it and all the privileges that came with it for a plate of food. He refused to consider the future, his descendants and the will of God upon His life.

Writing about Esau's actions, the author of Hebrews warns us to be careful not to be as irreverent as he was. He places Esau in a category alongside the sexually immorality (another sin that can easily ruin the destiny of a person).

> *See that no one is sexually immoral, or is godless like Esau, who for a single meal sold his inheritance rights as the eldest son. Afterward, as you know, when he wanted to inherit this blessing, he was rejected. He could bring about no change of mind, though he sought the blessing with tears.* - Hebrews 12:16-17

Immorality corrupts the spiritual formation of the person who engages in it. It amounts to seeking short-term pleasure at the expense of spiritual things and one's destiny. The Bible issues several warnings against sexual immorality because it is one of the favourite weapons of the devil when he wants to attack and ruin destinies.

> *Flee from sexual immorality. All other sins a man commits are outside his body, but he who sins sexually sins against his own body. Do you not know that your body is a temple of the Holy Spirit, who is in you, whom you have received from God? You are not your own; you were bought at a price. Therefore honour God with your body.* - 1 Corinthians 6:18-20

The Bible is clear that those who are immoral shall not inherit the kingdom of God. Their abominable actions disqualify them from dwelling in the presence of the Lord. Two Scriptures will suffice to reinforce this point.

> *Do you not know that the wicked will not inherit the kingdom of God? Do not be deceived: Neither the sexually immoral nor idolaters nor adulterers nor male prostitutes nor homosexual offenders nor thieves nor the greedy nor drunkards nor slanderers nor swindlers will inherit the kingdom of God.* - 1 Corinthians 6:9-10

> *But the cowardly, the unbelieving, the vile, the murderers, the sexually immoral, those who practice magic arts, the idolaters and all liars--their place will be in the fiery lake of burning sulfur. This is the second death."* - Revelation 21:8

This shows that besides hindering a person from attaining their destiny during their life on earth, immorality hinders them from reaching their eternal destiny. However, none of us has to live under the grip of the demons of sexual immorality.

There is a way out from this trap which is regular fasting to put the flesh under subjection so that the Spirit of God can be in supreme control in our lives.

The Scriptures are clear that the safest exit route from sexual sin is fleeing. To "flee" is to run away from a place or situation of danger. The Bible does not use this term by mistake because sexual sin is a dangerous trap of the enemy to ruin destinies. Joseph knew this and when he was tempted by Pharaoh's wife to have sexual relations with her, he fled (Genesis 39:12). He knew more than many people today that sexual sin is great wickedness and a sin against God (Genesis 39:9). His destiny was to be a great leader and the Lord had revealed this to him in dreams (Genesis 37:4-10). However, he had to walk in purity and holiness because these are the avenues of attracting and maintaining the favour of God in a person's life. Sexual purity is a spiritual exercise and it is impossible to live a life of purity without fasting. By the grace of God and through his commitment to live a life of holiness, Joseph was eventually elevated to leadership, just as God had intended (Genesis 41:42-43). He attained his destiny.

Like Joseph, we require spiritual empowerment to maintain spiritual discipline and eventually realise our destinies. Fasting will help us to keep a tight rein on our sexual desires so that we prevent them from leading us down the path to ruin.

Joseph'sself-controlandhisattainmentofgreatness as ordained by God can readily be compared and contrasted with Samson's recklessness and failure. Samson had been born and separated to God from his birth as a Nazirite. His purpose was to deliver Israel from the Philistines (Judges 13:5). However, he had a proclivity for indulgence with women. He let his sexual appetites run out of control and besides engaging in a relationship with Delilah (a Philistine), he also visited a prostitute (Judges 16:1). His uncontrolled desire for sexual pleasure cost him his destiny of being a deliverer. His lack of self-control cost him everything he had including his life. His example should serve as a warning to all of us not to let our carnal appetites rule over us at the expense of our destinies. Fasting helps to put the flesh where it belongs for our destinies to manifest. Therefore, it is necessary for all people of destiny.

The spirit might be willing but the flesh is often too weak. That is why Jesus commands us to watch and pray lest we succumb to temptations (Mark 14:38). Fasting as we pray makes our prayers more forceful and effective.

When believers fast and spend time with God in prayer, they activate divine power that helps them to turn down all forms of ungodliness, live in self-control and walk in purity.

> *For the grace of God that brings salvation has appeared to all men. It teaches us to say "No" to ungodliness and worldly passions, and to live self-controlled, upright and godly lives in this present age, while we wait for the blessed hope - the glorious appearing of our great God and Savior, Jesus Christ, who gave himself for us to redeem us from all wickedness and to purify for himself a people that are his very own, eager to do what is good.* - Titus 2:11-14

This grace of God is readily available to all believers irrespective of their background or denomination provided they are ready to meet the requirements that have been set in the Word for activating it. Fasting helps us to activate the fire of passion and a strong zeal for pleasing God, reinforcing the saints' blessed expectation of the Lord's imminent return.

The more a Christian is committed to fasting, the more the grace they receive to walk in purity and thus they move closer to activating the purposes of God in their lives.

God is holy and He expects nothing short of holiness from His people (1 Peter 5:5-6). This means that all those who desire to please Him and earn His approval must do all it takes to walk in the paths of holiness. More than anything else, fasting helps man to draw near to God. By going without food for some periods of time, man is able to physically demonstrate his commitment and

The more a Christian is committed to fasting, the more the grace they receive to walk in purity and thus they move closer to activating the purposes of God in their lives

desire to please God and do His will; a sizeable part of which includes manifesting one's destiny. Fasting is living by the Scripture that says *"man does not live by bread alone, but on every word that comes from the mouth of the Lord"* (Matthew 4:4).

The mistake that many people make today is similar to that of godless Esau. They love food more than they love their destinies. All believers should learn a great lesson from Esau's example and not love food more than their destiny. This will require that one exercise self-control. Fasting is a discipline for all followers of Jesus Christ, not just for ministers of the gospel. The Lord expects all believers to fast.

> *"When you fast, do not look somber as the hypocrites do, for they disfigure their faces to show men they are fasting. I tell you the truth, they have received their reward in full.* - Matthew 6:16

The Lord knows that without fasting, we are too weak to get hold of the spiritual blessings and privileges He has in store for us. Therefore, even if it is costly and causes some inconvenience, he calls on us to follow that path of self-discipline. The

Bible teaches on the need for all God's children to exercise discipline, even though it might not be easy or convenient to practice it.

> *No discipline seems pleasant at the time, but painful. Later on, however, it produces a harvest of righteousness and peace for those who have been trained by it.* - Hebrews 12:11

No believer should miss out on the rewards of blamelessness and tranquility that are promised to all those who exercise spiritual disciplines.

It was part of Esther's destiny to deliver the Jewish people from certain death. Some enemies of the Jewish people had made many plans on how to exterminate the race. However, Esther's cousin Mordecai deciphered that Esther could rescue her people by appealing to the king (Esther 4:14). Faced by this crisis, Esther called for a three day fast.

> *"Go, gather together all the Jews who are in Susa, and fast for me. Do not eat or drink for three days, night or day. I and my maids will fast as you do. When this is done, I will go to the king, even though it is against the law. And if I perish, I perish." So Mordecai went away and*

carried out all of Esther's instructions. - Esther 4:15-17

The will of God was that He would bring the Saviour of the world through the Jews. Yet, they were faced by the threat of annihilation because of the machinations of a man called Haman, who hated them. Their destinies as individuals and as a nation were threatened, and so they needed to act – and act fast. Their three-day fast opened a way for Esther to appeal to the king and her people were miraculously preserved. Their destiny was redeemed and their enemy was executed in their place. Fasting acted as a game changer in a time of deep crisis.

The Lord Jesus fasted for 40 days to fulfill His destiny upon the earth. Immediately after He emerged from the wilderness, He had clarity of His mission and purpose upon the earth which was already stated in the Scriptures by Prophet Isaiah.

"The Spirit of the Lord is on me, because he has anointed me to preach good news to the poor. He has sent me to proclaim freedom for the prisoners and recovery of sight for the blind, to release

> *the oppressed, to proclaim the year of the Lord's favour."* - Luke 4:18-19

Fasting is a strategy for fighting for one's destiny. Apostle Paul encouraged Timothy to wage spiritual warfare to his destiny in ministry so that he could become what the Lord has spoken of him in some prophetic words.

> *Timothy, my son, I give you this instruction in keeping with the prophecies once made about you, so that by following them you may fight the good fight.* - 1 Timothy 1:18

The word of God can guide you into fasting so that you can secure your destiny through spiritual warfare. All believers should do this because each person has a divine assignment they are meant to accomplish, whether they realise it or not. The Lord is gracious enough to reveal what our destiny is if we will enquire from Him during times of serious prayer and fasting.

Our personal destiny is closely connected to that of our land. The Lord calls on His people to pray for their land that it can be established in peace. He says that the prosperity of the land directly affects the individual well-being of the people. This kind of prayer would require to be accompanied by fasting to be effective.

> *Also, seek the peace and prosperity of the city to which I have carried you into exile. Pray to the LORD for it, because if it prospers, you too will prosper."* - Jeremiah 29:7

The importance of believers taking the destiny of their land seriously is demonstrated in the Bible by the elders on Elisha's day. They observed that their city Jericho, was in a favourable location but its water caused barrenness. They thus sought the help of a man of God.

> *The men of the city said to Elisha, "Look, our lord, this town is well situated, as you can see, but the water is bad and the land is unproductive." "Bring me a new bowl," he said, "and put salt in it." So they brought it to him. Then he went out to the spring and threw the salt into it, saying, "This is what the LORD says: 'I have healed this water. Never again will it cause death or make the land unproductive.'" And the water has remained wholesome to this day, according to the word Elisha had spoken.* - 2 Kings 2:19

The intervention of the servant of the Lord

caused the land to be healed because there is great power in the supernatural. We can appropriate such spiritual power by fasting and prayer. The stronghold of barrenness is not part of the plan God had in mind for His people and thus God's people need to confront it using spiritual force that can be obtained by fasting. In the same way, all the other works of Satan can bow at the saints who fast to seek divine power (Luke 10:19; 1 John 3:8b).

One of the greatest barriers we face as we move towards our destiny is the power of sin. Like Cain, we are constantly confronted by sin that is crouching at our door. God expects us to master it (Genesis 4:7). Fasting equips us to fight against the power of sin and iniquity. We have to put up a strong defense against the enemy and his schemes if we are to realise our destiny (James 4:7).

Our ability to fulfill the destiny God has in mind for us will depend to a great extent on how much we are willing to give up for our destiny. Part of what we must give up is food.

Chapter 3

FASTING IS A FORM OF WORSHIP

The Lord can do anything He desires but He cannot worship Himself. He has left that privilege and responsibility to man. God is Spirit and to worship Him acceptably, man must worship in spirit and in truth (John 4:24). This means that worship has to be heartfelt and has to originate from the deepest recesses of man's being. It must take into account our feelings, desires, appetites, hearts and minds. This also implies that we should be willing to lay down anything that has the potential of acting as a hindrance to our honouring God. This is where fasting comes in handy.

The word "worship" is rich in meaning and has several synonyms including reverence, honour, veneration, adulation, genuflection, devotion and glorification. It is a matter of one lowering themselves so that they can give credit to the one they worship. Worship is more of a lifestyle than of an event. It is an attitude of the heart that one adopts towards the Lord in which they regard Him with high honour and respect. Worship often includes bowing down in obeisance as an acknowledgment of God's power, glory, majesty, wisdom and authority. A true worshipper would be ready and willing to do anything the object of his worship demands even if that means going without food.

Some people have a hard time understanding worship because they think it refers to songs that have a slow tempo. The truth is that worship is not necessarily singing although singing is part of worship. Besides singing and making melody to the Lord, worship also entails spiritual acts such as offering our valuable possessions to God, offering one's body to serve God's purposes, and surrendering to the will of God even when it is inconvenient and costly.

The first commandment God gave His people touches on worship. He commanded them not to make for themselves any graven image with the intention of worshipping it. He says the reason He demands exclusive worship is that He is jealous. He does not want to compete with any other person or thing for man's worship.

> *"You shall not make for yourself an idol in the form of anything in heaven above or on the earth beneath or in the waters below.* - Exodus 20:4

We become true worshippers when we are willing to dethrone every other thing from our lives so that we can enthrone the Lord. This is not possible using human effort because the flesh stands in constant opposition to things of the Spirit.

> *The sinful mind is hostile to God. It does not submit to God's law, nor can it do so.* - Romans 8:7

The flesh is one of the strongest enemies of worship. Unfortunately, we do not have a way of avoiding it altogether because we need it to be alive on the earth. However, we can subdue it to conform to the will of the Spirit which desires to please God by offering Him acceptable worship. This is why fasting reinforces worship because it helps us to have the strength and willpower we need to resist bowing down to any other god but the Lord.

Genuine worship pleases the Lord and activates His power in the lives of His people. From the beginning, God desired that man would worship Him acceptably and He gave man instructions to that effect. He made this requirement known to the children of Israel through Moses.

> *Worship the LORD your God, and his blessing will be on your food and water. I will take away sickness from among you, and none will miscarry or be barren in your land. I will give you a full life span.* - Exodus 23:25-26

Worshipping God means giving Him due honour and attention, and that includes denying your body food and drink for some time so that your spirit man can tune into the heavenly frequency. Worship is necessary in the lives of human beings because it opens a door into the supernatural plane - the one that actually directs and controls everything that happens in the physical realm.

Yet another reason why fasting is an important and indispensable part of worship is that it is the pattern that Jesus Christ set for all His disciples. Jesus was fasting when He was confronted by the devil with a temptation to worship him (Matthew 4:9). His response was, "Away from me, Satan! For it is written: 'Worship the Lord your God, and serve him only'" (Matthew 4:10). Jesus shows us that God does

Worshipping God means giving Him due honour and attention, and that includes denying your body food and drink for some time so that your spirit man can tune into the heavenly frequency

not entertain divided attention or worship. He wants us to be sensitive to His requirements.

Franklin (2008) says that when believers fast, they become "amazingly sensitive to the things of God. As David stated, 'Deep calls unto deep' (Psalm 42:7)." This indicates that fasting pulls us into deeper fellowship, prayer, communion, love and Christlikeness. It is an act of worship that leaves an indelible mark on those who practice it.

Some worshippers in certain religions are willing to go to unimaginable lengths to show their commitment to their gods. Now that the God of the Bible is the only true God, His worshippers should not withhold anything when it comes to worshipping Him. Food is too little a thing to hinder a Christian from worshipping God. Each believer should therefore train themselves to fast.

Those who are unable to control their appetite for food are idolaters because they have made their stomachs their gods. In other words, they worship food instead of God. Apostle Paul makes mention of such people in his epistle to the church at Philippi.

Their destiny is destruction, their god is their stomach, and their glory is in their shame. Their mind is on earthly things. - Philippians 3:19

Having too much food and paying undue attention to the stomach can easily act as an impediment to worshiping the Almighty God.

One of the reasons why God delivered Israel is so that they might worship Him. He told Moses this much when He was commissioning him to deliver them from their bondage in Egypt.

And God said, "I will be with you. And this will be the sign to you that it is I who have sent you: When you have brought the people out of Egypt, you will worship God on this mountain." - Exodus 3:12

When Moses was disputing with Pharaoh concerning the release of God's people from the land of captivity, he mentioned that God wanted them set free so that they could worship Him.

Then the LORD said to Moses, "Go to Pharaoh and say to him, 'This is what the LORD says: Let my people go, so that they may worship me.
- Exodus 8:1

Part of the many acts of worship the Lord demanded from the children of Israel was fasting. On the Day of Atonement, He commanded that every Israelite to fast twenty four hours for their atonement.

> *"This is to be a lasting ordinance for you: On the tenth day of the seventh month you must deny yourselves and not do any work-- whether native-born or an alien living among you - because on this day atonement will be made for you, to cleanse you. Then, before the LORD, you will be clean from all your sins. It is a sabbath of rest, and you must deny yourselves; it is a lasting ordinance.* - Leviticus 16:29-31

The instruction to Israel to fast the whole day was meant to afflict their souls and show them their weakness and inability to help themselves. It was also an outward sign of their dependence on God. When one fasts, their bodies become weaker than they are when they are eating. This weakness helps to have a clear picture of oneself and of the God they worship.

God does not only take worship seriously but He also gives man clear instructions on how to worship

Him in a way that He will find acceptable. This is why all believers need to read and understand the Scriptures that command us to fast.

Fasting is a form of worship because it helps to dethrone unbelief. The only way to apprehend the things of God is by faith and any discipline that could help us to grow faith is a big blessing. We can see its significance through the example of Thomas who had strong unbelief in the resurrection of the Lord. He insisted he must see and touch His scars to believe that He was risen from the dead. When the Lord manifested Himself to him in a tangible way, his immediate action was that of worship.

> *Then he said to Thomas, "Put your finger here; see my hands. Reach out your hand and put it into my side. Stop doubting and believe." Thomas said to him, "My Lord and my God!"*
> - John 20:27-28

Thomas' unbelief would have been dealt a serious blow by fasting. The same is also true of the other disciples of Jesus. At some point, they were confronted by an epileptic spirit that they were unable to drive out from a boy. Embarrassed and defeated, they went to the Lord and asked

Jesus why they could not cast out that devil. He gave them a straightforward answer.

> *"However, this kind does not go out except by prayer and fasting."*- Matthew 17:21 (NKJV)

When we worship God with fasting, our spirits get in tune with Him and He gives us power to exercise dominion and authority over all the power of the enemy.

Fasting is also a form of worship because it pleases God by giving Him due reverence and awe. By such a sacrifice God is highly pleased.

> *Therefore, since we are receiving a kingdom that cannot be shaken, let us be thankful, and so worship God acceptably with reverence and awe.* - Hebrews 12:28

When the Lord is pleased by man's worship, He cannot withhold the riches of His glory and power. Therefore, fasting does not just make God happy but it also allows man an opportunity to receive from God.

One of the things that believers do when they fast is that they minister to the Lord. The disciples in the early church did this.

> *While they were worshiping the Lord and fasting, the Holy Spirit said, "Set apart for me Barnabas and Saul for the work to which I have called them."* - Acts 13:2

Ministering to the Lord implies a willingness to serve His need to be worshipped. When we meet this need, He opens more doors in our lives so that we can recruit others to join us in meeting it. That is why when the early church committed themselves to this work, the Holy Spirit spoke to them to set apart Saul and Barnabas for the divine assignment He had in mind for them. He wanted to send them on a mission to preach the gospel and win many converts so that worshippers could increase and cause the name of the Lord to be glorified.

When we worship God with fasting, our spirits get in tune with Him and He gives us power to exercise dominion and authority over all the power of the enemy

The Scriptures also teach that fasting is a higher form of worship. The willingness by man to lay aside food for some time indicates that their body, not just their spirit, is committed to God and to serving His purposes. Apostle Paul commands believers to offer their bodies as living sacrifices to God. The body also includes the stomach and its appetite for food.

> *Therefore, I urge you, brothers, in view of God's mercy, to offer your bodies as living sacrifices, holy and pleasing to God – this is your spiritual act of worship.* - Romans 12:1

Fasting is an outward demonstration of the posture of the heart – that of reverence and adoration. The idol worshippers recorded in the Old Testament give us a good example of this. Baal's prophets were not only willing to show reverence to their god by bowing down to it but also by offering their bodies to it even through painful exercises such as cutting themselves to the point of dripping blood (1 Kings 18:26-28). It is unfortunate that some followers of other religions are more disciplined in fasting than many Christians. It is this non-commitment that makes so many believers to be in continuous suspense, not sure what will happen next because their faith in the God they worship is shallow and wanting.

Fasting is indicating to God that you are nothing without Him. It is acknowledging your weakness and showing how desperately you need help from God. God rejoices in defending the weak and helping those who are humble enough to admit they need help. Wallis (1968) says that "fasting is a discipline of the body with a tendency to humble the soul."

The impact we make when singing is determined by how we have offered our bodies to God as living sacrifices. You will enhance your effectiveness as a servant of God if you combine it with fasting. It is surrendering your appetite to honour God. The same way believers are called to do away with fleshly desires, they also have to regularly give up their desire for food to practically demonstrate their allegiance to God.

Fasting is obedience to God's commands. A worshipper is required to revere and adore their object of worship. If Jesus is truly Lord in our lives, we should not avoid His command that we should fast. He says "when you fast," not "if you fast," indicating that He expects us to do it – and regularly (Matthew 6:16). The fact that He does not indicate how regularly believers should fast indicates that He has left the frequency to each believer as they shall be led by the Holy Spirit. His sheep know His voice and each worshipper should ask God how often and how long they should fast. The Lord provides His people enough grace to do all He has commanded them because His commands are not burdensome (1 John 5:3).

Every kingdom has a culture that guides it. Fasting is a kingdom culture. It is part of God's constitution that governs His kingdom. We cannot claim to worship God in spirit and in truth if our appetites for food have enslaved us. We cannot claim to be true disciples of Jesus if we accept everything else Jesus taught but turn down His teachings on fasting.

We cannot claim to worship God in spirit and in truth if our appetites for food have enslaved us

"When you fast, do not look somber as the hypocrites do, for they disfigure their faces to show men they are fasting. I tell you the truth,

> *they have received their reward in full. But when you fast, put oil on your head and wash your face, so that it will not be obvious to men that you are fasting, but only to your Father, who is unseen; and your Father, who sees what is done in secret, will reward you.* - Matthew 6:16-18

Besides underscoring the need for believers to fast, this Scripture also indicates that there are conditions God attaches to fasting for it to be an acceptable form of worship by the Father. It must not be done with ostentation in mind. Believers do not fast to make a name for themselves but to touch the heart of God by their humility and obedience. The full rewards of fasting are therefore going to escape those who do it to be seen by men. This shows that any act of worship that is done with the wrong motive is a loss to whoever practices it.

Fasting shows humility, seriousness and a desire for God to come into our lives and act in His mighty power. Elijah's fervent prayer at Mt Carmel was made in a posture of worship (1 Kings 18:36). Elijah's success in returning the Israelites back to the worship of the true God can be attributed to the fact he was a true worshipper. His worship consisted of fasting for forty days and forty nights (1 Kings 19:8). He took a position of giving birth where he let his innermost passions focus on God in prayer and got powerful results.

The Bible records that Elijah had a nature that is similar to ours in every way but he was able to act in the realm of the supernatural and produce great results. It takes a committed worshipper to pray in a way that can move the heavens (James 5:17-18). His example has significance in our lives because we can learn from his lifestyle of worship and reverence to God. This means that if we will engage in fasting to tune our hearts to God, we will receive extraordinary results like him. We can emulate his example of worship to God to elicit immediate responses from the throne room of heaven.

Chapter 4

SWIFTNESS IN THE SPIRIT REALM

The Bible compares the life of a Christian to a race. It is only the people who emerge first in a race that are awarded the winner's prize. This is why it is so important for each one of us to run their race in such a way that they will win the prize. To do that successfully, it is necessary for believers to do fasting. Fasting helps to cast aside spiritual weight that obstructs movement and sin that has the potential to encumber a person and hinder them from completing their race.

Therefore, since we are surrounded by such

> *a great cloud of witnesses, let us throw off everything that hinders and the sin that so easily entangles, and let us run with perseverance the race marked out for us.* - Hebrews 12:1

The word swiftness means "moving or capable of moving with great speed or velocity." If there is an area in which believers need to be swift, it is in their spiritual lives. The life of a believer is primarily a spiritual one. This means that anything they can do to stay light to be able to make progress is a great blessing that they should not despise. It should be the ambition of every believer to move with speed towards the attainment of the purposes of God in their lives.

Believers are pitted against a spiritual enemy called the devil and Scripture compares him to a roaring lion that is eagerly looking for some victim to devour (1 Peter 5:8). Just as it is in nature where lions make animals like zebras and antelopes their prey, the devil is determined to devour God's people. Just as healthy animals are able to run and escape being captured by lions, believers who have a healthy spiritual life and whose feet can run fast will be able to escape the grip of the evil one.

Some people make their journey towards their destiny at the speed of a tortoise and they unfortunately never get to their destination. It is the desire of the enemy to ruin as many souls as he can. On the other hand, the plan of God is that each man achieves their destiny without delay for His glory. That is where fasting comes in. Those who fast can lay aside every heaviness and impediment that could be sent into their lives to hinder them from fulfilling the purposes of God for their lives.

The spirit man in us has the potential to move faster than lightning but many of us are bogged down by doubt and unbelief while others are weighed down by food

The spirit man in us has the potential to move faster than lightning but many of us are bogged down by doubt and unbelief while others are weighed down by food. This is why believers should practice regular fasting so that they can become truly swift both in the natural and in the spiritual realms.

The Bible provides us with an example of a supernatural translation in Philip. After his encounter with the Ethiopian eunuch that led to the eunuch's conversion and baptism, Philip was suddenly caught away and swiftly transported by the Holy Spirit to Azotus to continue spreading the good news. It would have taken him a considerable amount of time for him to get there physically but the intervention of the supernatural led to his terrific speed in getting where God wanted him.

> *When they came up out of the water, the Spirit of the Lord suddenly took Philip away, and the eunuch did not see him again, but went on his way rejoicing. Philip, however, appeared at Azotus and travelled about, preaching the gospel in all the towns until he reached Caesarea.* - Acts 8:39-40

Jesus demonstrated the power and need for believers to have divine speed in one of His journeys with His disciples. The sea vessel they were travelling in got to its destination as soon as the disciples let Him in to ride with them.

> *Then they were willing to take him into the boat, and immediately the boat reached the shore*

where they were heading. - John 6:21

When believers fast, they let Jesus in to their circumstances and situations and He works powerfully to help them attain the supernatural. The same Holy Spirit that was working so powerfully in the ministry of Jesus and of the apostles is the same Holy Spirit that is in the church today. The difference between them and us is that many people today are not fully surrendered to His power and guidance, so they miss the supernatural that should be a part of their daily lives.

The eagle is known for its swiftness (Job 9:26; Deuteronomy 28:49). The Lord uses it as a metaphor to refer to His people and how He renews the strength of those who hope in Him.

> *He gives strength to the weary and increases the power of the weak. Even youths grow tired and weary, and young men stumble and fall; but those who hope in the LORD will renew their strength. They will soar on wings like eagles; they will run and not grow weary, they will walk and not be faint.* - Isaiah 40:29-31

One of the strongest indicators that one is

hoping in the Lord is willingness to forsake all else including food to seek His face. When believers fast to express their hunger and desire for God, He makes them get spiritual strength to rise above the storms of life like eagles. God gives them the strength to run without growing tired and walk without becoming exhausted. God is delighted to make the feet of His people like those of a deer.

When believers fast to express their hunger and desire for God, He makes them get spiritual strength to rise above the storms of life like eagles

He makes my feet like the feet of a deer; he enables me to stand on the heights. - Psalm 18:33

One major reason why believers need to pursue swiftness in the spirit realm through fasting is that the king's business requires haste. There is so much the King of kings and Lord of lords desires to have accomplished within a short time if we will let Him do it through us.

"the king's business required haste." - 1 Samuel 21:8b

Fasting was the last step in Jesus' journey to ministry. One of the many things it did in His life is that it gave Him spiritual swiftness. He did not have too much time to do what the Father had sent Him to do. Thus, He had to make the most of the three years He had to complete His earthly ministry. He needed divine speed to be effective. In that time, He performed many instant miracles and healings. Three examples will suffice.

> *Then the woman, seeing that she could not go unnoticed, came trembling and fell at his feet. In the presence of all the people, she told why she had touched him and how she had been instantly healed.* - Luke 8:47

> *Jesus reached out his hand and touched the man. "I am willing," he said. "Be clean!" Immediately he was cured of his leprosy.* - Matthew 8:3

> *Seeing a fig tree by the road, he went up to it but found nothing on it except leaves. Then he said to it, "May you never bear fruit again!" Immediately the tree withered.* - Matthew 21:19

These instances demonstrate that when one is appropriately divinely positioned, he or she can be a vessel that causes supernatural things to happen with swiftness. Fasting is a way of becoming a vessel of noble use that the Lord is looking for to co-work with in His kingdom. It helps to cleanse one's spirit from ordinary things and to set himself apart for God's purposes (2 Timothy 2:20-21). These purposes include offering help to those who are weak, encouraging the discouraged, comforting the grieving and proclaiming deliverance to the captives (Luke 4:18-19). Believers who have sharpened their spiritual senses with fasting find it easy to flow in the gifts of the Spirit because they are alert and connected to the move of God.

Believers who have sharpened their spiritual senses with fasting find it easy to flow in the gifts of the Spirit because they are alert and connected to the move of God

The apostles also engaged in fasting and like the Lord, they became swift in the miraculous works they performed. For instance, Peter and John walked in the supernatural with great efficiency and ease when they encountered the forty-year old crippled beggar at the Beautiful Gate.

> *Taking him by the right hand, he helped him up, and instantly the man's feet and ankles became strong.* - Acts 3:7

There are many things God desires to do with swiftness – and finality - if He would find ready and willing vessels. Like the disciples in the early church, believers today can increase their spiritual speed by taking regular times of fasting so that they can be fully aligned to the purposes of God. That way, they can have ease discerning what God is doing and partner with Him to produce tangible results in the lives of His people.

Fasting increases our sensitivity to the move of God so that we can tell where He is moving towards. The Bible teaches that those who are born again move like the wind

> *The wind blows wherever it pleases. You hear its sound, but you cannot tell where it comes from or where it is going. So it is with everyone born of the Spirit."* - John 3:8

Fasting is an avenue of activating the supernatural resources of heaven that are packaged in the gifts of the Spirit. These can help us achieve results in a way that is many times faster than using only human methods and techniques.

Take the example of the disciples and their miraculous catch of fish. It is recorded thus:

> *When he had finished speaking, he said to Simon, "Put out into deep water, and let down the nets for a catch." Simon answered, "Master, we've worked hard all night and haven't caught anything. But because you say so, I will let down the nets." When they had done so, they caught such a large number of fish that their nets began to break. So they signaled their partners in the other boat to come and help them, and they came and filled both boats so full that they began to sink. When Simon Peter saw this, he fell at Jesus' knees and said, "Go away from me, Lord; I am a sinful man!" For he and all his companions were astonished at the catch of fish they had taken.* - Luke 5:4-9

What the disciples could not accomplish overnight they did in one casting of the net at Jesus' word. This can be the case in the many impossible situations that believers face if they would be willing to seek the voice of God in fasting. Many people have wasted much valuable time and effort labouring without profit because they are unable or are unwilling to seek the Lord with fasting. The realm of the spirit has potentialities that ordinary man can only faintly think about. When the Lord brings spiritual swiftness, He accompanies it with great productivity and profit. This is why it is so important to seek to have spiritual swiftness even if that will require us to abstain from food for some time.

Many people have wasted much valuable time and effort labouring without profit because they are unable or are unwilling to seek the Lord with fasting

Just as in the natural where when the axe is dull it requires much effort, the spirit man requires much effort to achieve any results when he is bogged down with food and other hindrances. Those who are wise sharpen the inner man through fasting and they can save a lot of energy in accomplishing tasks in their lives.

If the ax is dull and its edge unsharpened, more strength is needed but skill will bring success. - Ecclesiastes 10:10

When disciples get in tune with the supernatural, they begin to walk in miracles, signs and wonders. The disciples worked closely with the Lord to bring instant deliverance.

She kept this up for many days. Finally Paul became so troubled that he turned around and said to the spirit, "In the name of Jesus Christ I command you to come out of her!" At that moment the spirit left her. - Acts 16:18

Swiftness is not limited to spiritual speed. It also entails physical haste. One of the strongest examples of a man moving in a supernatural speed is that of Elijah. After the epic contest at Mount Carmel in which the prophets of Baal were slaughtered (1 Kings 18:40) and rain fell after three and a half years of drought, the Lord gave Elijah's feet divine swiftness to run faster than a chariot.

The power of the LORD came upon Elijah and, tucking his cloak into his belt, he ran ahead of Ahab all the way to Jezreel. - 1 Kings 18:46

This extraordinary strength was only available and possible to Elijah, who was a true worshipper of God. It enabled him to run many miles ahead of Ahab's horse-drawn chariot. He included fasting in the spiritual disciplines he observed as recorded in 1 Kings 19:8.

This kind of supernatural speed is the one the Lord wants to use in dealing with wickedness in these last days. He promises to act with rapidity in releasing judgment upon the wicked who stand opposed to His purposes.

> *And the offerings of Judah and Jerusalem will be acceptable to the LORD, as in days gone by, as in former years. "So I will come near to you for judgment. I will be quick to testify against sorcerers, adulterers and perjurers, against those who defraud laborers of their wages, who oppress the widows and the fatherless, and deprive aliens of justice, but do not fear me," says the LORD Almighty.* - Malachi 3:4-5

The Lord will not come to the earth in person to act with haste against the wicked. He has for the time being delegated that duty to His servants and He wants them to submit to His will. When they take the posture of humility and submission, He can back up their acceptable worship so that He can decisively destroy the works of the enemy. Servants of God can tune themselves into His working by engaging in fasting so that they are able to discern where He wants to act next. The Son of God was manifested to destroy all the works of the enemy (1 John 3:8) and this can be fast tracked by believers when they engage in fasting with this understanding.

Fasting facilitates spiritual swiftness by giving human beings control over their spirit man. It enables one to sharpen their spiritual focus. It does this by helping a person to subdue the flesh and it becomes so easy to hear God. The Scriptures illustrate this using Elijah's example.

> *The LORD said, "Go out and stand on the mountain in the presence of the LORD, for the LORD is about to pass by." Then a great and powerful wind tore the mountains apart and shattered the rocks before the LORD, but the LORD was not in the wind. After the wind there was an earthquake, but the LORD was not in the earthquake. After the earthquake*

> *came a fire, but the LORD was not in the fire. And after the fire came a gentle whisper.* - 1 Kings 19:11-12

Just like Elijah heard God's voice with clarity when he was fasting, it is easier for us to hear the voice of the Lord when we are fasting than when we are not. The removal of all hindrances to the voice of God enables us to connect with speed with the heavenly Father.

Believers should not make any mistake on this matter. The Lord desires that they become swift both in the physical and in the spiritual realms. Through fasting, it becomes easier for followers of Jesus to connect with speed with what God is doing and what He is planning for the future.

> *Do you not know? Have you not heard? The LORD is the everlasting God, the Creator of the ends of the earth. He will not grow tired or weary, and his understanding no one can fathom. He gives strength to the weary and increases the power of the weak. Even youths grow tired and weary, and young men stumble and fall; but those who hope in the LORD will renew their strength. They will soar on wings*

like eagles; they will run and not grow weary, they will walk and not be faint. - Isaiah 40:28-31

The Lord is delighted to have His children partake in the divine nature and has provided everything they need for life and godliness (2 Peter 1:3-4). Therefore, the same way He is as swift as an eagle, He wants His children to have divine speed in all they do. He does this by removing their weakness and replacing it with His strength and by increasing the ability of His people to endure the challenges of life with divine help. That way, His people stand out from the crowd and are able to do the extraordinary in His name.

In one of his many Psalms, David extolled the Lord because he knew that He avails strength to him to help him do the remarkable.

It is God who arms me with strength and makes my way perfect. He makes my feet like the feet of a deer; he enables me to stand on the heights. He trains my hands for battle; my arms can bend a bow of bronze. - Psalm 18:32-34

The same strength and ability to do great things with speed that God availed to David is available to all saints today who will seek His face. Those who indicate their seriousness in this matter with prayer and fasting stand a better chance of receiving it than those who merely hope or believe that this power will be made available to them without showing their desperation for it.

Indeed as Solomon says, the race is not necessarily won by the physically swift. (Ecclesiastes 9:11). However, believers who are empowered by the Holy Spirit are going to do mighty things by God's power. The things of the Kingdom are not for the physically strong but for those who will rely on the power and wisdom of God in the person of the Holy Spirit.

The things of the Kingdom are not for the physically strong but for those who will rely on the power and wisdom of God in the person of the Holy Spirit

> *So he said to me, "This is the word of the LORD to Zerubbabel: 'Not by might nor by power, but by my Spirit,' says the LORD Almighty.* - Zechariah 4:6

We can receive more of this divine power to

make us swift in all we do through fasting. We can also increase our swiftness in doing the assignment the Lord has given us by fasting so that our inner being can receive more of the divine power to wage warfare against the powers of darkness. Believers already have God's power delegated to them by Jesus Christ.

> *I have given you authority to trample on snakes and scorpions and to overcome all the power of the enemy; nothing will harm you.* - Luke 10:19

We can become swifter in attacking the camp of the enemy and destroying his works by committing ourselves to the discipline of regular fasting.

Spirits of delay, stagnation, roundabout, procrastination and other time wasters are favourite weapons of the devil to interfere with the speed of God's people. Believers can wage warfare against these wicked spirits and emerge victorious especially when they combine their prayers with fasting.

Chapter 5

FASTING BUILDS YOUR SPIRIT

The world in which we live demands a certain degree of forcefulness because it is a battlefield, not a playground. Those who are weak and beggarly are bound to suffer loss in a war zone. This means that believers need to take all the necessary steps to build up their inner man. We need to build our spirits to be able to stand a fighting chance in this world that is populated by hostile and opposing forces.

Fasting is one of the most effective ways of

building our spirit man. To do this, we need to understand that man is a spirit being that has a soul and lives in a body (1 Thessalonians 5:24). The same way man is born as an infant with little physical strength, he is born a weak spiritual creature. He needs to take spiritual nourishment for his spirit to grow. That spiritual nutrition includes the reading and meditating on the word of God, prayer, fellowship and fasting.

Many of the things God wants to give His children as an inheritance have been possessed by the devil who is the god of this world (2 Corinthians 4:4). It takes a person with a strong spirit to confront and defeat the enemy and thus wrestle the inheritance out of his hands.

We can glean a lesson on this from the example of the nation of Israel. The Israelites had to fight and dispossess their enemies to possess the Promised Land. Many of the tribes they were to fight against were way stronger than they and yet God required them to wage war against them. The need for them to build up their spiritual muscles was aggravated by the fact that some of the people in the enemy tribes were giants (Numbers 13:34). In more or less the same way, we also have spiritual enemies such as principalities and strongholds that might seem as giants to us. This makes the need to fast an urgent requirement for us as we wage warfare against them.

It requires a considerable amount of forcefulness to attain any spiritual progress and to walk with God. The devil fights fiercely to hinder the blessings that God has released from reaching us. The Scriptures give us an example of this in the answer to Daniel's prayers that was withheld by the Prince of Persia for twenty one days after the answer was released from heaven.

> *Then he continued, "Do not be afraid, Daniel. Since the first day that you set your mind to gain understanding and to humble yourself before your God, your words were heard, and I have come in response to them. But the prince of the Persian kingdom resisted me twenty-one days. Then Michael, one of the chief princes, came to help me, because I was detained there with the king of Persia.* - Daniel 10:12-13

By practicing fasting, Daniel took a posture of

a spiritual wrestler. His constant prayers coupled with fasting tilted the scales in his favour in the angelic realm. Angel Michael, a warrior angel, was consequently released to contend with the prince of Persia. Eventually, the host of holy angels won the battle and Daniel was able to receive the answers to his prayers.

The unseen realities of warfare in the spirit realm make it necessary for God's people to combine their prayer with fasting. Fasting is a divinely ordained weapon of vanquishing the forces of evil that stand opposed to the purposes of God in the lives of His people.

The devil is a spiritual being and he has some measure of spiritual strength. Ephesians 2:2 describes him as "the ruler of the kingdom of the air." This should help us to understand that although we are more than conquerors in Christ

Fasting is a divinely ordained weapon of vanquishing the forces of evil that stand opposed to the purposes of God in the lives of His people

Jesus (Romans 8:37), we have an enemy who has some spiritual muscles he flexes against God's people alongside his army of demons. All believers need to build their spirit man to understand the full implications of spiritual warfare because it is an inevitable component of the life of faith. This kind of spiritual formation and growth cannot be complete without fasting.

We can learn this from the example of Jesus and the temptations He faced and conquered in the wilderness while fasting at the beginning of His ministry. The devil had the temerity to tempt Jesus to worship him because he holds a certain amount of control over the unredeemed world (Matthew 4:8-9). Many people have been deceived by the evil one to pursue shortcuts to wealth because they do not know how to get hold of divine wealth by laying claim to the promises of God. Those who have declared their faith in Jesus must pursue spiritual building by fasting so that they can become a formidable force against the onslaught of the enemy.

The kingdom of God is not advanced by

weaklings. It demands spiritual force. Jesus underscored this point as He was talking about how it has been advancing since the days of John the Baptist.

> *From the days of John the Baptist until now, the kingdom of heaven has been forcefully advancing, and forceful men lay hold of it.* - Matthew 11:12

The Bible uses several examples to depict the church as an army. Each spiritual soldier needs to build their spiritual muscle so that when the day of evil comes, they can stand firm and not be overwhelmed. This is one of the many reasons why Apostle Paul taught about spiritual warfare. He insisted on the need for believers to be built up so that they can stand the test of warfare that is certain to come to each of them.

> *For our struggle is not against flesh and blood, but against the rulers, against the authorities, against the powers of this dark world and against the spiritual forces of evil in the heavenly realms. Therefore put on the full armor of God, so that when the day of evil comes, you may be able to stand your ground, and after you have done everything, to stand.* - Ephesians 6:12-13

To emerge victors in this battle, all believers need to build their spirit man by putting on the full armour. These are spiritual garments that touch on one's character, not their outward appearance. They include righteousness, salvation, faith, the word, a readiness to preach the gospel of peace as well as prayers on all occasions (Ephesians 6:13-18).

Christian living is a demanding spiritual exercise that requires zeal, commitment and discipline. Just the same way professional wrestlers work out regularly to tone their muscles as they prepare for competitions; believers have to "work out" in the spirit so that they will be in good spiritual shape when warfare emerges. The enemy believers are fighting against is not physical so their physical credentials might not add them much value in this spiritual contest. Thus, for us to wage this warfare successfully, believers need to be spiritually sound, sober and alert. This is why we have to exercise our spirits to make it fit for this battle. Fasting helps us to keep our spirits in shape especially when it is combined with all manner of prayers and petitions.

> *And pray in the Spirit on all occasions with all kinds of prayers and requests. With this in mind, be alert and always keep on praying for all the saints.* - Ephesians 6:18

This prayer that Paul recommends for all followers of Jesus cannot be effective without fasting. Praying in the Spirit on all occasions is one of the quickest ways to build oneself up in the most holy faith.

> *But you, dear friends, build yourselves up in your most holy faith and pray in the Holy Spirit.* - Jude 1:20

The word of God is indispensable in building our spirit and increasing our faith in God. It is the fuel that powers our inner man to propel us towards more godliness and effectiveness.

When we fast and devote the time we would have spent eating in prayer, the Word and meditation, the precious truths that are locked up in the word of God begin to become alive in our lives. They are activated and they begin to change us from inside out. That way, our faith grows. In return, we receive the power we need to work great exploits in faith because nothing is impossible for the man who has faith.

> *"Everything is possible for him who believes."* - Mark 9:23b

The life of a true believer is a matter of faith from start to finish. The more we interact with God through fasting, the more we are able to grow in our dimensions of encounter with Him. We are consequently able to move from the shallow waters of faith into the great depths of intimacy with God through the Holy Spirit. In those profound levels, the supernatural becomes our portion because our spirit man is built up into a stature that can readily receive from God (See Ezekiel 47:1-5). In addition, we are able to put our carnal nature subdued under God's power. The sinful nature is a big enemy of spirituality so it must be

> ***The word of God is indispensable in building our spirit and increasing our faith in God. It is the fuel that powers our inner man to propel us towards more godliness and effectiveness***

put in its place by fasting.

The sinful mind is hostile to God. It does not submit to God's law, nor can it do so. - Romans 8:7

The flesh consistently opposes the spirit and they are in an incessant battle. We are the ones to decide who between them will prevail. If we want the spirit man to win, we can fast to reinforce his strength but if we want the flesh to win, we can wine and dine with liberality and he will win with ease. Food is a wonderful blessing but it is often an enemy of spiritual growth and maturity.

There are evil desires that wage war against our spirits (1 Peter 2:11). When we build our spirits through regular fasting, they become more like God and they are able to turn down the devil and his evil suggestions.

A weak spirit cannot successfully resist temptation as the Lord requires of us in Mark 14:38. Prayer reinforced with fasting increases our chances of emerging victorious in the spiritual arena. The devil is a ruthless enemy and desires to sift God's people like wheat. Prayer and fasting will abort his plans and if the temptations come, the extent of the damage they cause will be scaled downwards if we have fasted to pray about them. Jesus assured Peter that he would be delivered from his hour of trial because He had already prayed for him that his faith would not fail (Luke 22:31-32). This privilege is available to us as well. If we build up our spirit man, we will be able to go into the future and destroy or altogether abort the schemes of the enemy against our lives and those around us.

Fasting makes us to tune to the frequency of the Spirit so that we can receive spiritual gifts to enable us to do the supernatural. Those who have walked with God and allowed the Holy Spirit to build His treasures into them easily receive and manifest spiritual gifts that God has given the church to help her in accomplishing the supernatural. It is easier for a person whose spirit is built up to walk in the gifts of power, utterance and revelation (1 Corinthians 12:7-10). Spiritual building heightens one's perception, understanding, patience and zeal, making them effective and truly productive.

Fasting helps believers to develop a militant

spirit so that they do not give up easily. The Bible describes God as "a man of war" (Exodus 15:3) and we are meant to emulate Him. The same way Israel needed physical strength to pull down the altars of idols that other tribes had put up (Deuteronomy7:5), we need spiritual strength to pull down the unseen works of the enemy. Fasting is one of the divinely ordained disciplines of hardening the spirit man.

> ***Fasting helps believers to develop a militant spirit so that they do not give up easily... It is one of the divinely ordained disciplines of hardening the spirit man***

Our bodies are the temples of the Holy Spirit. We must prepare for Him a dwelling environment that is conducive by doing away with all the things He does not want. That demands some considerable level of determination. That is why we need to fast regularly so that we can detect the spiritual magnitude of the enemies we face because the flesh cannot assess them accurately. Spiritual matters are only understood by the spiritual man (1 Corinthians 2:14).

One truth about God is that He often leaves some enemies in the lives of His people so as to help them build their spiritual capacity and teach them warfare. The same way soldiers are trained in harsh conditions before being sent to battle zones, the Lord often spares an enemy or two in the lives of his followers to teach them war. He also left some few of those enemies to train the Israelites battle (Judges 3:1-2). God often leaves some problems in our lives so that in fighting them we can build our inner man by prayer and fasting. Jesus assured His disciples that He would not eradicate tribulation from their lives. Their presence is an avenue for them to experience firsthand the peace that only He can give.

One truth about God is that He often leaves some enemies in the lives of His people so as to help them build their spiritual capacity and teach them warfare

> *"I have told you these things, so that in me you may have peace. In this world you will have trouble. But take heart! I have overcome the world."* - John 16:33

Troubles and tribulations are not enjoyable to the natural man. The Bible however instructs us to "consider it pure joy, my brothers, whenever you face trials of many kinds, because you know that the testing of your faith develops perseverance" (James 1:2-3). It describes diverse trials as the path to spiritual maturity and completeness because the working out of patient endurance in one's life causes them to build their spirit man.

> *Perseverance must finish its work so that you may be mature and complete, not lacking anything.* - James 1:4

Followers of Jesus need to have formidable spirits that know nothing about giving up no matter what happens. Like the Lord, they need to have a fighting spirit that is not cowed by challenges or hardship. The Bible describes the Holy Spirit as a fighting Spirit.

> *Yet they rebelled and grieved his Holy Spirit. So he turned and became their enemy and he himself fought against them.* - Isaiah 63:10

We can emulate His character trait of a fighter. Individuals who patiently develop a fighting spirit stand a high chance of sailing through the adversities that are bound to come their way in life with grace and maturity. These things cause the name of the Lord to be glorified. Their character resembles that of Job who, instead of complaining and cursing God when he was severely tested glorified, worshipped and praised His name (Job 1:20-22). The Lord is highly pleased by such people.

One of the titles of God is Jehovah Sabaoth - the Lord of hosts (Zechariah 8:1-2). "Hosts" is an old English word for armies. As believers in Jesus, we have His DNA. Therefore, we should have strong spirits just like His. If you are born of God, you must be a person of warfare. It is necessary to mention that this warfare is not physical but spiritual.

It is in times of fasting that God teaches our hands to do battle. We receive the divine might we need to subdue our enemies when we express our dependence on the Lord by laying aside our routine for some time to grow in communion with Him in fasting.

> *Praise be to the LORD my Rock, who trains my hands for war, my fingers for battle. He is my loving God and my fortress, my stronghold and my deliverer, my shield, in whom I take refuge, who subdues peoples under me.* - Psalm 144:1-2

God is not pleased by cowards. Those who do not take time to fast to build their spirits cannot get hold of the promises of God both in this life and in eternity. The Bile states with clarity that cowards will not inherit the kingdom of God. They will be damned alongside the immoral, worshippers of idols, sorcerers, liars and magicians.

> *But the cowardly, the unbelieving, the vile, the murderers, the sexually immoral, those who practice magic arts, the idolaters and all liars - their place will be in the fiery lake of burning sulfur. This is the second death."* - Revelation 21:8

Fasting equips believers with the willingness, energy, zeal and passion to fight for their destinies. It helps us to deal with complacency, non-commitment and spiritual coldness that are the bane of the success of the spiritual lives of so many people. It does this by enabling them to put on the full armour of God especially the shield of faith to quench the fiery darts of the enemy and the Sword of the Spirit, which is the word of God. This is why the Lord commands us to let His word abide in us in generous quantities.

> *Let the word of Christ dwell in you richly as you teach and admonish one another with all wisdom, and as you sing psalms, hymns and spiritual songs with gratitude in your hearts to God.* - Colossians 3:16

Believers who take in the word of God by reading and meditating on it as they fast have the privilege of seeing the word work in their lives as a fire and a hammer (Jeremiah 23:39). These two can be used to destroy the works of the devil and to build the work that the Lord wants built up and established.

> ***Fasting helps believers to become figures of authority in the spirit realm and empowers them to exercise the authority He has delegated to them***

When you continually build your spirit with regular fasting, you adopt the face of the Son of God who is the Lion of the tribe of Judah

(Revelation 5:5). The lion is the king of the jungle and is famed for its bravery. Fasting helps believers to become figures of authority in the spirit realm and empowers them to exercise the authority He has delegated to them. Fasting also helps you not to give up easily by training your spirit to become militant. It helps you to have inner reinforcement against discouragement which is a very strong weapon in the armoury of the enemy.

Fasting helps to build your spirit man so that you do not give up on these three things.

1. Yourself

Abstaining from food to seek God helps believers to keep moving forward because they know that the one who began the good work in them shall bring it to accomplishment (Philippians 1:6). It helps them to fight against sin, evil and impurity with passion because they recognise that they are the tools of the enemy to destroy the lives of God's people. Fasting helps someone to maintain the faith that God will help them however difficult the circumstances in their life might become.

It puts believers in the ranks of the people who break through in life. People who make it in life are not angels. Like Elijah, they have flesh and blood and are subject to the passions all human beings face (James 5:17-18). His lifestyle of fasting helped him to stand firm for God's purposes in the face of still opposition from the prophets of Baal and he prevailed. Fasting strengthens believers so that even when they have been given a knockout by the enemy in the spiritual battlefield, they drag themselves back into the ring before the referee blows the whistle.

2. Your Possessions

One of the best examples of why we should not give up on our possessions is that of David in 1 Samuel 30:1-20. After the siege at Ziklag, he pursued the enemies with the little strength he still had left. The result was that the Lord helped him to recover everything he had lost including his wives, the young, the old and all the plunder (v.18). He did not allow his human weakness to stand in his way of getting back what was legally his because he depended on the unlimited strength of the Lord.

Fasting will help you not to give up on your children, husband, business, health, career, ministry, calling, generational problems as well as your eternal destiny. Fasting helps one to retain hope and faith which are very important virtues in the lives of God's people.

It is our duty and inheritance as priests and kings in God's kingdom to fight His battles (1 Peter 2:9). Believers are a royal priesthood. The work of kings is to lead their people to battle to conquer other nations. In many nations of the world, the president is the commander-in-chief of the armed forces. God is our commander and we are His troops. Jesus has gone ahead of us to make a way for us to follow. Many of the things God

> ***Many of the things God has promised His children are in the hands of the enemy. Believers who fast reinforce their spirits to fight for their inheritance which includes God's promises to you***

has promised His children are in the hands of the enemy. Believers who fast reinforce their spirits to fight for their inheritance. This inheritance includes the promises God has made to you.

When we fast, we invite the Lord to fight for us the same way He promised to fight for Israel (Deuteronomy 1:29-30). The Lord goes ahead of you to fight for you on condition that you will arise. If you just remain seated, He will do nothing and you lose your property and inheritance.

3. Your God

The worst thing that can happen to a human being is to lose their faith in God. Such an action has both temporal and eternal consequences and we should avoid it with all our might. The discomfiting truth is that Satan will raise a strong opposition against our relationship with God. The Bible commands us to resist Him with steadfastness and he will flee.

> *Submit yourselves, then, to God. Resist the devil, and he will flee from you.* - James 4:8

Fasting helps us to stay on course in faith because

spiritual things do not always happen at the speed of lightning. It often requires persistence and endurance to get hold of the promises of God.

> *We do not want you to become lazy, but to imitate those who through faith and patience inherit what has been promised.* - Hebrews 6:12

Fasting helps to build both faith and patience into one's life which are of far greater value than the nourishment one might get from food.

Chapter 6

DETOXING OUR BODIES AND SPIRITS

Pollution is one of the greatest problems of our day. It has caused numerous problems that have affected many people around the world. In the same way natural waste causes environmental pollution, there is a possibility of the human body and spirit being polluted by food substances. To detox is to abstain from or rid the body of unhealthy substances. Detoxing is a scientifically proven way of improving one's physical and spiritual health. Fasting helps in this process because it entails giving up food and drink for some time because some food items contain poisonous substances. It helps the human body to get rid of both physical and spiritual toxins.

Some of the problems that come as a result of the accumulation of toxins in the body include feeling sluggish, lethargic and developing skin glitches. These toxins can cause both short-term and long-term problems and that is why there is need to deal with them decisively through fasting.

Ormatian (1999) writes about the efficiency of fasting in detoxing by describing the process she calls "cleansing power fasting" in these terms:

> Cleansing Power Fasting is a cleansing process from beginning to end. It cleanses your spirit, soul, mind, and body all at the same time. Physically, our bodies are constantly eliminating poisons through the lungs, skin, bowels, and kidneys. In fact, our bodies are going through miraculous processes every day, and fasting provides the most favorable conditions under which to accomplish these things. When you fast,

> the body is free to do the thing it does best, which is a natural self-healing and cleansing process. When you aren't filling the body with food for a period of time, all the energy that is usually used to digest, assimilate, and metabolize is now spent in purifying the body.

Food is habitual and our bodies can so become accustomed to it to a dangerous level – almost to the enslaving level of an addiction if we are not careful. Just the same way some people are addicted to drugs, others are addicted to food. One of the best ways to avoid food addiction is committing oneself to regular fasting. The cleansing it avails is very precious and is readily available to all believers and produces good physical and spiritual results especially if it is done in the right way.

Believers practice fasting primarily as a spiritual discipline but they derive manifold blessings from it. The Bible is emphatic that believers need both spiritual and physical exercises although it states that spiritual exercises have a more lasting value than physical ones.

For physical training is of some value, but godliness has value for all things, holding promise for both the present life and the life to come. - 1 Timothy 4:8

When believers engage in fasting, they train their spirits to have ease in relating with God. The hidden man of the heart is able to flex his unseen muscles and provide much needed illumination to the course of life of that person. The Bible says that the Lord uses the spirit of man as His lamp to access man's inner being.

The lamp of the LORD searches the spirit of a man; it searches out his inmost being. - Proverbs 20:27

This shows the need for both the inner and outer man to be subjected to discipline and training which yields good results. Any discipline that would help a man have a stronger relationship with God is a great blessing.

The word of God teaches that the body is the temple of the Holy Spirit. As such, it is His dwelling place. That makes it necessary for us to keep the body in a state that is habitable for the

Holy Spirit, whose most prominent character trait is holiness. He cannot abide in a place or body that is polluted or corrupted.

> *Don't you know that you yourselves are God's temple and that God's Spirit lives in you?* - 1 Corinthians 3:16

Talking about the body as God's dwelling place, Apostle Paul emphasises that God's people need to treat it with due care and consideration to avoid letting it get bogged down by sin. Jesus warned His followers against being weighed down by gluttony and drunkenness because they render people spiritually insensitive (Luke 21:34). Some sins such as immorality not only have an impact on the body but are also harmful to a man's spirit. The word of God says that a man who engages in sexual relations with a harlot becomes one spirit with her. In this case, a physical action leads to spiritual defilement.

> *Do you not know that he who unites himself with a prostitute is one with her in body? For it is said, "The two will become one flesh." But he who unites himself with the Lord is one with him in spirit. Flee from sexual immorality. All other sins*

> *a man commits are outside his body, but he who sins sexually sins against his own body. Do you not know that your body is a temple of the Holy Spirit, who is in you, whom you have received from God? You are not your own; you were bought at a price. Therefore honor God with your body.* - 1 Corinthians 6:16-19

This Scripture underscores the need for believers to fast to get rid of the spiritual toxins of lust and desires for immorality that can easily poison one's soul and body and lead them to sin. Fasting helps to keep fleshly appetites under control to prevent the body from leading the spirit to filth. As long as someone is in the flesh, these desires can arise. This makes the need to practice fasting regularly even more pressing.

> ***Fasting helps to keep fleshly appetites under control to prevent the body from leading the spirit to filth***

Fullness of food dulls a person's spiritual senses. Many of the abominations that are done on the earth today are done by people whose bellies are full and whose spirits are cluttered by the toxins of godlessness and sin. Like Sodom of old, those who engage in perversions are usually overfed and care little about righteousness and fairness. They are haughty and have no sense of reverence and this causes them to act as beasts.

> *"'Now this was the sin of your sister Sodom: She and her daughters were arrogant, overfed and unconcerned; they did not help the poor and needy. They were haughty and did detestable things before me. Therefore I did away with them as you have seen.* - Ezekiel 16:49-50

Like the disciples of Jesus whose senses were sometimes dulled by the toxin of unbelief, we can become hard of hearing when our stomachs are too full (Matthew 13:15). Unbelief is a close companion of gluttony and greed. Being dull of hearing indicates becoming lazy in the things of the Spirit. It also means sluggishness or indolence. It is about laziness in learning the word of God. It is a threat to many people who desire to please God.

Fasting is clearing the clutter of the flesh so that God can move in your life with ease. The flesh has many desires for evil. Those who allow their carnal mind to reign in their lives risk destruction (Galatians 6:7-8). This is why those who desire to please God are encouraged to sow to the Spirit. This includes, but is not limited to, fasting. When a believer takes time to fast, they suppress their carnal appetites. In fact, when most people fast, their physical bodies become weak, and they cannot easily use them in sins such as immorality in that weakened physical state. This is why regular fasting is so crucial in the lives of God's people because it helps them to tame their ungodly desires. Apostle Paul reiterates this point:

> *Those who live according to the sinful nature have their minds set on what that nature desires; but those who live in accordance with the Spirit have their minds set on what the Spirit desires. The mind of sinful man is death, but the mind controlled by the Spirit is life and peace; the sinful mind is hostile to God. It does not submit to God's law, nor can it do so. Those controlled by the sinful nature cannot please God.* - Romans 8:5-8

When believers spare time to fast, they avail themselves to God for a time of divine encounters because they remove all forms of opposition and resistance. They eradicate spiritual and physical toxins, thus making it relatively easy for them to have visions, dreams, hear God, pray and breakthrough more effectively.

The Bible gives a clear illustration of this truth through the life of Jesus Christ. It was only when He was led by the Holy Spirit into the wilderness to fast that the unseen realities of the spirit world became tangible and practical experiences in His life. The devil followed Him into the wilderness specifically to tempt Him to sin. After He conquered the temptations Satan brought His way, there was a break as the devil went away to wait for another opportune moment (Luke 4:13). The devil uses the same strategy against us and we must watch out lest he outwits us.

An important thing we need to know is that when we fast, we do not do it to change God; it changes us to be like Him. Hagin (1981) says, "You're not going to move God. He doesn't move. He's already prone to do certain things, and He's going to do them just as soon as you get in contact with Him and let Him." Ignorance of this truth is a dangerous trap that hinders God's people from enjoying the benefits of fasting when they do it from a point of ignorance. Regular fasting sharpens one's spiritual senses making it easy for them to perceive that their fasting will change them rather than change God. This is why one should feast on the Word and on godly teachings as they fast.

when we fast, we do not do it to change God; it changes us to be like Him

Food is a heavy load in our bodies and some of its remnants can remain in our stomachs for very long. The cleansing of physical toxins from our bodies can be facilitated by taking lots of water when one is fasting. Ormatian believes that "fasting is the only way to get rid of certain poisons." She adds, that for those who "have taken a lot of drugs like aspirin, tranquilizers, pain killers, antibiotics, and others, fasting is a good way to rid yourself of the leftover residue that will still be floating around in your system." This helps to decongest the body which leads to a better health. The body derives much pleasure and gets an opportunity to rest and rejuvenate when one takes only water.

Spiritually, fasting helps to eradicate the toxin of pride. Wallis (1968) observes that "Pride and a too full stomach are old bedfellows. Fasting, then, is a divine corrective to the pride of the human heart." Believers who fast are able to replace pride with humility and thus they position themselves in a place where they can receive God's grace. The Lord has said that He resists the proud but generously gives grace to the humble (James 4:6).

There are many reasons why we need to detox our bodies. Ormatian observes that certain habits such as taking too much food, failing to exercise, stress, poor feeding habits, forgetting to drink water, not taking in enough air and sunshine and not resting enough allows the blood to accumulate toxins. She adds that the blood must be clean to keep disease from finding breeding ground. When someone who is fasting deliberately practices healthy living habits, they become better people spiritually and physically because they remove from their lives contaminants that could easily function as the breeding ground for sicknesses. She recommends that one should take a fast when they feel a minor illness coming on. This helps to prevent its progress by giving the body an opportunity to concentrate on the process of self-healing and cleansing.

The Bible is God's manual for our lives. It says man cannot live by bread alone but by every word that proceeds from the mouth of God (Matthew 4:4). This clearly shows that depending on physical food alone for sustenance can easily act as an impediment to the spirit man. Individuals who do not fast have a difficult time perceiving spiritual matters because they are best understood by men whose spirits are alive to God (1 Corinthians 2:14).

Individuals who do not fast have a difficult time perceiving spiritual matters because they are best understood by men whose spirits are alive to God

Among the other physical benefits of fasting taught in the Bible is that it is a powerful tool in fighting the aging process. The Bible describes numerous physical and spiritual benefits of this discipline in Isaiah 58. It says that when an individual fasts, they become like a garden that is supplied with generous amounts of water.

> *The LORD will guide you always; he will satisfy your needs in a sun-scorched land and will strengthen your frame. You will be like a well-watered garden, like a spring whose waters never fail.* - Isaiah 58:11

As would be expected, a well-watered garden is pleasant to look at and has lush vegetation. Those who fast keep the aging process under control. Fasting helps the body to get rid of old cells and generate new ones. Body toxins hinder this process so getting rid of them through fasting does a lot of good to the body. Ormatian says that fasting arrests the process of aging, makes a person become more attractive and helps them to feel better spiritually, mentally and physically. She says that each day of the fast, the spirit, soul and body become increasingly cleaner. She adds that fasting is a very rapid way to make the body release toxins and thus, no person should view it as starvation of the body. It is a time of both rest and rejuvenation. In addition, fasting helps in strengthening the bones by revitalising their strength.

The Lord promises to supply strength to those who hope in Him. The strength He gives is not just spiritual; there is a physical dimension to it as well (Isaiah 40:28-31). When we fast, we receive the willpower we need to resist spiritual and physical toxins because fasting enables us to take control of what happens to us. We are able to withstand spiritual battles when our spirits are alert and vigilant.

Just like eagles who take time to go to secluded places and abstain from food to rekindle their youth and get a new lease of life, believers can take regular times of fasting to get rid of worn out tissues and spiritual muscles and receive new ones. Fasting helps someone to break old spiritual habits that can easily lead to spiritual complacency. The word of God promises children of God these benefits as part of the redemption package.

Praise the LORD, O my soul; all my inmost being, praise his holy name. Praise the LORD, O my soul,

> *and forget not all his benefits - who forgives all your sins and heals all your diseases, who redeems your life from the pit and crowns you with love and compassion, who satisfies your desires with good things so that your youth is renewed like the eagle's.* - Psalm 103:1-5

The package that the Lord offers His people consists of both physical and spiritual components. Forgiveness offers cleansing from spiritual toxins as does love and compassion that eradiate rejection and desperation. On the physical front, the Lord provides healing for diseases which can waken and slow down the body as well as deliverance which secures our lives from the onslaught of the enemy. The redeemed of God should therefore not hesitate to do all in their power to activate this package, even if that means going on periods of fasting.

All believers who are willing to pay the price of going without food for some time are going to enjoy the massive benefits of releasing both physical and spiritual toxins from their lives. Their lives are going to be better for it. The inconveniences one might experience while fasting are a small price to pay compared to the benefits that believers get when they detox their bodies and spirits.

Chapter 7

FASTING PRODUCES DEATH THAT PRODUCES POWER

It is paradoxical that death can produce power yet this is true of fasting. Most people see death as a purely negative thing but the Bible depicts it differently. The death that comes as a result of practicing the discipline of fasting is not physical but is a condition of the heart in which one gives up all their rights and claims for the sake of the Lord and His kingdom. Believers can gain precious treasures that include God's immeasurable power by surrendering their lives to His purposes. The willingness to lay down one's life leads to a life of superior quality that is characterised by the fullness of God's power and great fruitfulness. The word of God commands all followers of Jesus to die to self so that they can live for Him. While teaching this, Jesus uses the example of grain of wheat which cannot be fruitful unless it dies.

> *I tell you the truth, unless a kernel of wheat falls to the ground and dies, it remains only a single seed. But if it dies, it produces many seeds. The man who loves his life will lose it, while the man who hates his life in this world will keep it for eternal life.* - John 12:24-25

The same way a grain of wheat remains solitary before it dies but multiplies when it is planted and grows to yield a harvest, our lives will never make spiritual meaning if we do not deliberately die to all our selfish ambitions. Jesus underscores the fact that those who selfishly cling to their lives end up hurting instead of benefitting themselves. Only the people who are willing to acknowledge that they are weak and helpless without God's help can be truly productive in His kingdom.

Jesus teaches this idea time and again as He does in this Scripture:

> *Then he said to them all: "If anyone would come after me, he must deny himself and take up his cross daily and follow me.* - Luke 9:23

In the Roman Empire, the cross was the choice tool of execution for law breakers. Anyone who was condemned to die had to bear his own cross and transport it to the place where he was to be executed. Those who carried the cross publicly demonstrated their willingness to be associated with a certain cause and showed a readiness to die for what they held dear to their hearts. Believers today have to do the same thing. They will not bear a physical cross but they have to willingly participate in all the spiritual disciplines Jesus has commanded

The same way a grain of wheat remains solitary before it dies but multiplies when it is planted and grows to yield a harvest, our lives will never make spiritual meaning if we do not deliberately die to all our selfish ambitions

His disciples. The very same way Jesus carried His cross to Golgotha, we have to carry ours and follow Him every day. This includes willingly subjecting ourselves to the discipline of fasting as He has commanded.

We cannot merely call Jesus 'Lord, Lord,' and yet do not do what He commands (Luke 6:46). Doing that amounts to mocking His authority and taking the work He did on the cross for granted. The word of God does not give suggestions but commands. Thus, when we make the mistake of disregarding the commands, we show that we are irreverent and self-willed. Jesus has commanded those who desire to be His followers and friends to be willing to die to all selfish ambitions so that His life and supernatural power can find true expression in their lives. By dying to personal ambitions and desires that lurk

We cannot merely call Jesus 'Lord, Lord,' and yet do not do what He commands (Luke 6:46). Doing that amounts to mocking His authority and taking the work He did on the cross for granted

within our being, we demonstrate our readiness to live for God's glory. Apostle Paul showed the significance of this by commanding all the children of God to put to death all the works of the flesh that include immorality, sinful desires, moral corruption and self-indulgence.

> *Put to death, therefore, whatever belongs to your earthly nature: sexual immorality, impurity, lust, evil desires and greed, which is idolatry.* - Colossians 3:5

These things are enemies of spiritual living and progress. We need to deal with them forcefully and with great determination lest they lead to our downfall. They are dangerous because they compete with God for our attention. Their only solution is death and hence the need for each child of God to carry their cross daily as they follow Jesus.

Fasting is willingly submitting to physical weakness so that the immeasurable power of God can manifest in your life. Until we are fully dead to self, we cannot hope to please God. God is not delighted by those who live for themselves, their appetites, ambitions, likes and concerns. In His eyes, those who do so are idolaters and they are condemned unless they repent. It is an unwise thing to worship one's ambitions which are temporary at the expense of the Almighty God.

When we fast, we starve to the power of the sinful nature in us. This helps to create room for God's power to manifest in us in an expansive way. God delights in showing His mighty power in situations where human weakness is most pronounced. Until man comes to an end of himself and his means, the power of God cannot manifest in and through him. This truth is best taught in the word of God by the example of Apostle Paul. He had a thorn in the flesh that caused him much distress by exposing his helplessness as a man. He sought the Lord to help remove the problem but instead of removing it, the Lord told him that His power is made perfect in weakness.

Until man comes to an end of himself and his means, the power of God cannot manifest in and through him

> *But he said to me, "My grace is sufficient for you, for my power is made perfect in weakness." Therefore I will boast all the more gladly about my weaknesses, so that Christ's power may rest on me. That is why, for Christ's sake, I delight in weaknesses, in insults, in hardships, in persecutions, in difficulties. For when I am weak, then I am strong.* - 2 Corinthians 12:9-10

By His answer to Apostle Paul, the Lord demonstrated that His power is particularly effective when human beings realise their weakness and inability to help themselves. This means that anything that could cause a man to come to an end of himself and acknowledge God's power is a wonderful blessing. The reason why many people do not experience the supernatural in their lives is not that God is weak or unwilling to manifest His power to them. It is that they are often too strong-willed and self-sufficient to leave any room for God's power. Apostle Paul knew that the things that expose us to suffering, weakness and even death are the very channels through which God gets an opportunity to show His might in our lives. We would do well to learn from his experience with that oppressive thorn.

As children of God, we should not see the things that expose our helplessness as disadvantages but as opportunities for the advancement of the kingdom of God and its interests. The safest way out of weakness is to admit one's powerlessness and seek divine help. That way, the weaknesses we are all prone to having can become our greatest sources of strength when we yield them to the Lord. Fasting is the route to follow to die to self so that God's power can come through for us.

As indicated by the response that the Lord gives Apostle Paul, God's power rests on His people in the form of the grace of Jesus Christ. The Lord tells Paul, "My grace is sufficient for you." God avails His manifold grace through His beloved Son Jesus. Indeed, all grace and truth are found in Christ (John 1:17). By taking our time to fast, we take a posture in which God can consider us in His mercy and avail the unmerited favour we need to go through the demands and vicissitudes of life without fear and with power. The Lord invites us to His throne from where we can receive both mercy and grace to help us demonstrate His power through our weaknesses.

> *Let us then approach the throne of grace with confidence, so that we may receive mercy and find grace to help us in our time of need.* - Hebrews 4:16

Every believer who will recognise the position of Jesus as a High Priest and seek His help through fasting (and prayer) is bound to receive it. God is faithful to His word and keeps each promise He has made to His people. He invites His people to ask, seek and knock, promising to respond favourably to all those who do one or more of these things (Matthew 7:7-8). He is delighted to reward all who seek Him diligently. He is predisposed to come to the aid of those who realise that without His power, they are as good as dead. Indeed, Jesus teaches that we cannot do anything of our own because the power we need for productivity is vested only in Him.

> *Remain in me, and I will remain in you No branch can bear fruit by itself; it must remain in the vine. Neither can you bear fruit unless you remain in me.* - John 15:4

Apostle Paul advanced the idea of dying to all selfish ambition further as he was writing to the saints in Galatia. He indicated to them that by virtue of his decision to follow Christ and serve him with all he had, he had come to a point where nothing else mattered to him. He was no longer living to fulfill his ambitions but purely for the glory of God. In other words, he was as good as dead to his own interests, desires and dreams.

> *I have been crucified with Christ and I no longer live, but Christ lives in me. The life I live in the body, I live by faith in the Son of God, who loved me and gave himself for me.* - Galatians 2:20

Fasting is bringing your flesh to a point of death where you can begin to have inner spiritual power. The flesh is in constant competition with the spirit man and the Lord knows that when we fast, we deny it the power to rule over us and direct the course of our lives. The only way to do that is by killing its many wild desires. Many people make the mistake of trying to cast out the flesh instead of crucifying it. Colossians 3:5 commands us not to entertain it but to "put to death" all the things that belong to the earthly nature. To see the power of God working through us, we must remove all spiritual impediments from our path by dealing decisively with the flesh and its evil appetites. We have to subdue it to a point where it is dead so that God's life, which is full of supernatural power, can find expression through us. Denying the body the very thing it desires most is one of the most effective ways of telling it that the spirit man is in control in our lives. That is why fasting is an effective way of disciplining the flesh.

By fasting, we identify with the death of Jesus Christ and fellowship with Him in His sufferings. If Jesus had not died, He would not have been glorified. Without glorification, He would not have become the Saviour of the world. Jesus had to face death to disarm the devil who held power over death (Hebrews 2:14-15). In the same way, we cannot enjoy the fullness of the power and glory of God in the flesh without crucifying it.

> ***Denying the body the very thing it desires most is one of the most effective ways of telling it that the spirit man is in control in our lives***

Fasting causes our desires of self-preservation to fade into insignificance and as this happens, we open ourselves up to more of God's fullness in our lives.

When we follow in Jesus' footsteps and die to self like Him, we receive the power of the Holy Spirit to enable us to do great exploits. This is the pattern the Lord has set for His people. The early disciples willingly lay down their lives for Jesus and for the gospel and they consequently did many signs, miracles and wonders when the Spirit of God rested on them. They abandoned their careers and trades for the sake of the gospel and committed themselves wholly to a life of the Word, prayer and fasting (see Acts 2:46-47 and 6:2). As a result, the Lord released great power into their lives and they walked in extraordinary miracles.

On one occasion, they were asked how they were able to perform great miraculous works. The response was: *"It is by the name of Jesus Christ of Nazareth…that this man stands healed"* (Acts 4:10). The act of the disciples of Jesus of abandoning their careers and businesses for the sake of the kingdom of God was equivalent to dying because it meant they had given up all their interests for the Lord. Unlike their peers, they lived for God, not their personal ambitions, pursuits and careers. As a result, the Lord was delighted to demonstrate His supernatural power through their ministries by working mighty signs and wonders. Their death to their personal ambitions released the power of God both to themselves and to those they ministered to. The more they became committed and sold out to the gospel, the greater the measure of God's power they enjoyed.

We cannot live in the flesh and in the Spirit at the same time. The two are in constant opposition and are irreconcilable (Romans 8:8-9). One has to die for the other to prevail. Those who kill the former give an opportunity for the latter to manifest His wonder-working power and this causes God to be truly glorified.

The fullness of God's power was demonstrated by the death and resurrection of Jesus Christ. His example demonstrated that resurrection begins where death ends because He cannot die again. Like Him, once we die to self, we have nothing to fear because we have already been translated into eternal life. This gives us life that is truly life, empoweredandsustained by the supernatural. Concerning this truth, Jesus says, "Whoever lives and believes in me shall never die" (John 11:26). With this kind of hope and assurance, a believer can live with unmistakable boldness for they know they are safe for all eternity as long as they remain within the confines of the word of God. They can stand against any challenge and obstacle and defeat it through the indefatigable power of the Holy Spirit.

We cannot live in the flesh and in the Spirit at the same time. The two are in constant opposition and are irreconcilable (Romans 8:8-9). One has to die for the other to prevail

In an anticipatory way, death is swallowed up in victory as a believer seeks God with fasting. The Bible foretells a time when death shall be dealt a final blow when the Lord shall return (1

Corinthians 15:54). It also shows that the victory over death is already ours because of the power of the Holy Spirit that works in us. The more yielded to God a believer becomes, the more the measure of His power they manifest in their life, ministry, career and calling.

A follower of Jesus has to give himself or herself to this kind of death that produces power and life. The same way Jesus laid down His life for us on His own accord (John 10:18), believers emulate Him when they give up food for His sake and for His eternal kingdom. That includes submitting to Christian disciplines so that they can get something more important from Him – His power in them. This is a great treasure that all believers need to comprehend because it is the power of Christ that abides in Him that gives His followers the hope of sharing in His eternal glory (Colossians 1:27).

When one is truly dead to self, evil desires and all manner of sin, they begin to manifest the power of God in their life. This is the example that Jesus set for His followers when He went to the cross to bear their punishment. In his humanity, he had a desire to go on living and to escape that punishment and even told the Father to remove the cup from Him (Matthew 26:39). However, it was not the Father's will that He should escape it. Jesus thus chose to submit and said, "Yet not my will, but yours be done" (Luke 22:42). Jesus submitted to the Father's will and was consequently glorified. Believers receive the same reward when they fast in the Father's will. Food is a wonderful blessing that God has given His children for their nourishment. However, He requires them to forfeit it so that they may grow in communion with Him and do His perfect will for them. That communion generates spiritual power that helps them to accomplish what nothing else can.

Fasting helps someone to remove every sense of entitlement to self so that Jesus can live in and through them. That way, they become a treasure in the kingdom of God. The Lord says that He is going to manifest Himself to all who love Him and keep His word (John 14:21-23). When the Lord manifests Himself to a person in the fullness of His power, impossibilities turn into possibilities and

His power becomes evident in all such a person does. Fasting makes one lose what is limited and temporary so that they can gain what is unlimited and eternal.

Fasting also is showing that someone loves God more than anything else and that they are ready to submit to Him to the point of enduring hardship for His sake. If you are willingly to give yourself over to the kind of death that comes by fasting, you position yourself to become a vessel of honour that God can use for every good work.

Fasting makes one lose what is limited and temporary so that they can gain what is unlimited and eternal

> *In a large house there are articles not only of gold and silver, but also of wood and clay; some are for noble purposes and some for ignoble. If a man cleanses himself from the latter, he will be an instrument for noble purposes, made holy, useful to the Master and prepared to do any good work.*
> - 2 Timothy 2:20-21

Many people have missed their path of

fruitfulness and usefulness in the things of God because they failed to subdue their appetite for food. The presence and power of God are not easily carried by people who do not willingly offer themselves to die for the sake of their faith. It demands that we deny ourselves, our rights, feelings, ambitions and comforts so that we can become carriers of the power of God. That kind of death prepares us to be custodians and partakers of the supernatural.

Moses experienced this firsthand when he ascended the mountain of the Lord to receive the law God had for His people. After a time of separation from the people, he returned full of the glory of God and heavenly power so that it became needful for him to cover his face with a veil whenever he was talking to the children of Israel (Exodus 34:33-35). Moses recounts that the reason why the power of God rested on him so gloriously when he went to the mountain to receive the commandments from God was that he was in a period of intense fasting. He records that he fasted for forty days on two occasions.

> *When I went up on the mountain to receive the tablets of stone, the tablets of the covenant that the LORD had made with you, I stayed on the mountain forty days and forty nights; I ate no bread and drank no water. Then once again I fell prostrate before the LORD for forty days and forty nights; I ate no bread and drank no water, because of all the sin you had committed, doing what was evil in the LORD's sight and so provoking him to anger.* - Deuteronomy 9:8, 19

The sacrifice that Moses offered to God by going without nourishment for his body enabled him to represent Israelites before God by interceding for them and by acting as their intermediary. Many of them were not in a condition in which they could approach God directly because of their many sins that would easily have led to their destruction. Moses could however present their case before God because he was His chosen mediator and he knew how to approach God with fasting so that His power could be manifested through him.

Fasting also helps you to set aside your human credentials so that you can rely on the Holy Spirit. You consider your intelligence, high education and human effort "dead" so that you can rely on the supernatural intelligence of the Holy Spirit in your life, ministry, career etc. The word of God states that we are all weak and we need help from God's Spirit (Romans 8:26). Indeed, the human mind, will, emotions and heart are too weak to do anything worthwhile for God on their own accord. When we relinquish our lives to the leadership of the Holy Spirit, we become channels through which God can show forth His great power to the world. The Holy Spirit is a reliable guide because He knows all the things God has freely given us including His mighty power that is at our disposal (1 Corinthians 2:10-12).

the depth of the human soul is powerfully affected by the work of the cross if we fully die to self and live for God. The more you die to self, the more alive you become in Christ

The Holy Spirit helps us to access new realms of God's power when we reinforce our prayers with fasting. There are certain levels of faith and conviction that we cannot attain without fasting.

This means that the depth of the human soul is powerfully affected by the work of the cross if we fully die to self and live for God. The more you die to self, the more alive you become in Christ. Apostle Paul demonstrates this by the kind of life he lived and by his unshakeable commitment to the work of the ministry. He said his life was worth nothing in his estimation and all that really mattered was his testimony of God's grace to as many as God wanted him to reach (Acts 20:24). This unwavering commitment can be traced back to the beginning of his ministry where he did an absolute fast for three days immediately after his conversion (Acts 9:9).

Jesus instructs His disciples not to live as pagans. This implies that they are not to run after temporary things such as food, clothing and shelter as worldly people do. Instead, He commands them to seek first His kingdom and His righteousness (Matthew 6:25-34). Putting the kingdom of God above all else necessitates regular fasting to activate the spirit realms. The coming of His kingdom into their lives avails the power necessary to meet all their needs. That way, God's power manifests in their lives in a great way. On the other hand, those who are not fully sold out to God and His kingdom waver and turn away to chasing the things of this world that do not truly satisfy. It is therefore necessary that each follower of Jesus gets their priorities right if they desire to see the life of God manifested in their lives.

Fasting is a needful discipline for those who would become useful in God's kingdom. Jesus calls upon us to consider ourselves dead to the sinful nature and its passions and desires (Galatians 5:24). That is a command each disciple must take personally and seriously. Those who think they have all the life and power they need miss out on Him and the mighty power He wants to release into their lives for His glory.

Chapter 8

FASTING IS A SACRIFICE

Human beings cannot worship God in an acceptable way without offering sacrifices to Him. The Bible teaches that believers should offer different types of sacrifices. These include such things as giving to the Kingdom, yielding their bodies for holy purposes, thanksgiving and fasting.

To sacrifice is to surrender something precious, desirable or of value for something that is considered to be more valuable or more precious. When believers fast, they willingly lay aside food that could benefit their bodies temporarily so that they can connect with God and receive divine power to help them in their spiritual lives. There is no end to the benefits they can receive when they set themselves to worship God sacrificially in this way.

Fasting is a good way of touching God's heart because it touches a person's innermost being. Human beings need food, clothing and shelter as basic needs for living. When one chooses to go without one of these, they demonstrate a willingness to forego a desirable thing so that they can reinforce their worship. God is just and He looks at such people with favour and rewards them generously. The Bible says that God is not unjust to forget the labour of His people (Hebrews 6:10). Therefore, those who commit themselves to glorifying Him in this manner receive rewards from Him.

Every sacrifice has a voice. Laying aside food and drink for some time as a way of honouring and seeking God speaks before Him in a manner that nothing else can. The Bible teaches that the blood of Jesus speaks. Not only does it have a voice but it also speaks better things than the blood of Abel.

> *...to Jesus the mediator of a new covenant, and to the sprinkled blood that speaks a better word than the blood of Abel.* - Hebrews 12:24

By His sacrificial death on the cross, Jesus entered into the presence of God with His blood and secured man's redemption from sin and the captivity of the devil. Unlike the blood of goats and bulls that was offered in the old covenant that was not effective in bringing salvation, the blood of Jesus brings redemption to mankind if they approach God by faith. It speaks forgiveness, redemption, mercy, grace, acceptance and eternal life.

> *He did not enter by means of the blood of goats and calves; but he entered the Most Holy Place once for all by his own blood, having obtained eternal redemption. How much more, then, will the blood of Christ, who through the eternal Spirit offered himself unblemished to God, cleanse our consciences from acts that lead to death, so that we may serve the living God! In fact, the law*

requires that nearly everything be cleansed with blood, and without the shedding of blood there is no forgiveness. - Hebrews 9:12, 14, 22

The blood of Jesus is the only sacrifice God accepts for man's sins. The Lord demands death as the punishment for sin and thus Jesus' sacrificial death earned the people who will believe reconciliation and eternal life. The redemption story does not however end there. The Lord requires His followers to offer appropriate sacrifices, which include fasting, as they continue on the path of salvation. The same way Jesus gave up His divine privileges as the creator of the universe and died on the cross to atone for our sins, we follow in His footsteps of selflessness and doing the Father's will when we fast. God is pleased by such sacrificial acts of obedience.

Fasting is also humbling oneself before the Lord. The Bible gives an example of King Ahab who fasted to humble himself before God. It describes him as a man who had sold himself over to wickedness egged on by his wife Jezebel. His sins reached the highest heavens because he indulged in idolatry which displeased the Lord greatly. God decided to release judgment upon him for his great wickedness. However, when Ahab knew that the Lord was planning to bring disaster on him and his household because of his sin, he decided to fast and humble himself before the King of kings.

> *(There was never a man like Ahab, who sold himself to do evil in the eyes of the LORD, urged on by Jezebel his wife. He behaved in the vilest manner by going after idols, like the Amorites the LORD drove out before Israel.) When Ahab heard these words, he tore his clothes, put on sackcloth and fasted. He lay in sackcloth and went around meekly. Then the word of the LORD came to Elijah the Tishbite: "Have you noticed how Ahab has humbled himself before me? Because he has humbled himself, I will not bring this disaster in his day, but I will bring it on his house in the days of his son."* - 1 Kings 21:25-29

By offering a sacrifice of humility and penitence before God, Ahab was able to forestall God's judgment. His humility and willingness to lay down his ego and every sense of self-importance attracted divine mercy into his life and he was spared from calamity. His submissive surrender to God gave all glory to God and activated divine mercy. When the Lord is touched by the fasting of His people, He releases favour, mercy, blessing, peace, forgiveness and exaltation which are of superior value to the food believers might forgo to offer this sacrifice.

Fasting is also divinely ordained way of humbling oneself before the Lord (Psalm 35:13b). It touches the heart of God when human beings, who are very weak compared to God's great power and self-sufficiency, bow before Him in sacrificial worship as they fast. The word of God says that "God opposes the proud but gives grace to the humble (James 4:6). Instead of relying on their limited understanding and strength, human beings who fast express their dependence on God. They sacrifice their ego and self-importance and this

When the Lord is touched by the fasting of His people, He releases favour, mercy, blessing, peace, forgiveness and exaltation which are of superior value to the food believers might forgo to offer this sacrifice

pleases God. It causes Him to be gracious towards them. All the food in this world would not be enough to pay for an ounce of God's grace because it is priceless. It is a heavenly resource that all the wealth in this world cannot purchase. This is why God gives His grace as a free gift because no man can pay for it. Fasting helps believers to draw near the throne of grace with confidence from where they can obtain mercy and find grace to help in the time of need.

> *Let us then approach the throne of grace with confidence, so that we may receive mercy and find grace to help us in our time of need.* - Hebrews 4:16

An important thing to note about fasting is that it is surrendering oneself wholeheartedly to the will of God. It is not twisting the hand of God so that He can do what He does not want. Rather, it is yielding to Him so that His will for your life and destiny can be fulfilled. This is what happened to the people of Nineveh when God sent the Prophet Jonah to warn them of the looming judgment. When their king got that news, he commanded the people to go without food so that they may implore God for forgiveness and mercy. This act made the Lord to become favourably disposed towards them.

> *On the first day, Jonah started into the city. He proclaimed: "Forty more days and Nineveh will be overturned." The Ninevites believed God. They declared a fast, and all of them, from the greatest to the least, put on sackcloth. When the news reached the king of Nineveh, he rose from his throne, took off his royal robes, covered himself with sackcloth and sat down in the dust. Then he issued a proclamation in Nineveh: "By the decree of the king and his nobles: Do not let any man or beast, herd or flock, taste anything; do not let them eat or drink. But let man and beast be covered with sackcloth. Let everyone call urgently on God. Let them give up their evil ways and their violence. Who knows? God may yet relent and with compassion turn from his fierce anger so that we will not perish." When God saw what they did and how they turned from their evil ways, he had compassion and did not bring upon them the destruction he had threatened.* - Jonah 3:4-10

The people of Nineveh sacrificed their food, time, honour and dignity so that they could fast and seek God's mercy. They also gave up the desires of their flesh as well as the evil ways and the violence they had been enjoying so that they could call on God to spare them and their city. Their king also gave up his impressive royal robes and the expensive and delicious meals that are served in king's palaces so that he could seek God who would spare them from destruction that God was planning to release upon them. Their sacrifice touched God's heart and caused Him to spare them the calamity He had planned.

Fasting is a sacrifice that brings revival in the lives of God's people. Their commitment to go without bodily nourishment results in something of a higher value in spiritual reawakening that brings peace, joy, salvation, restoration, oneness, harmony and God's favour. In the days of Prophet Joel, the Lord called His people to a time of fasting so that they could mend their broken relationship with Him. The Lord wanted all His people to forego all comforts and temporary pleasures for the sake of their relationship with Him which is of far greater value than anything else. Two examples of such divine invitations of Israel to fast in the days of Joel will suffice.

> *Declare a holy fast; call a sacred assembly. Summon the elders and all who live in the land to the house of the LORD your God, and cry out to the LORD.* - Joel 1:14

> *'Even now,' declares the LORD, 'return to me with all your heart, with fasting and weeping and mourning.' Blow the trumpet in Zion, declare a holy fast, call a sacred assembly.* - Joel 2:12, 15

The willingness of the people of Israel to honour God's call to a solemn assembly was an indication that they value their relationship with Him and His purposes for them more than they value food and drink. Foregoing temporary gratification for God's eternal purposes is an act of sacrifice that touches and glorifies God.

Foregoing temporary gratification for God's eternal purposes is an act of sacrifice that touches and glorifies God

Fasting is also a sacrifice because it entails knowing the will of God and doing it to glorify Him. The body is the most precious sacrifice God wants from us. His word tells us to prioritise offering our bodies to Him so that He can find a holy dwelling place in us. He knows that when He has the body, He has access to everything else that we can ever lay claim to.

> *Therefore, I urge you, brothers, in view of God's mercy, to offer your bodies as living sacrifices, holy and pleasing to God - this is your spiritual act of worship.* - Romans 12:1

Man is a triune being that consists of a spirit, soul and a body. The spirit and the soul are tenants in the house we describe the body. This house is temporary, but the spirit and soul it hosts are eternal because they are made in the image of God who cannot die. Therefore, God wants us to surrender our bodies to Him as a matter of priority because when we do that, we become truly spiritual. We open ourselves up to His holiness and in that way; we can offer acceptable sacrifices and glorify Him according to His will for us.

Besides subjecting the body to the authority of the Lord, fasting also helps to submit everything believers own to the Lordship of Jesus. Genuine believers engage in fasting as a way of obeying the commands of the Lord. The body is the vessel that carries the heart and flesh of man and could easily find enjoyment in the fleeting pleasures of sin, which are enjoyable to some degree, especially to the carnal man. When a believer decides to forego these temporary joys for the sake of eternal life and for living a godly life that has promise for this life and for the one to come, they glorify God in a great way. Apostle Paul commands all saints to give up all indecency, participation in orgies as well as drinking of intoxicating drinks, negative emotions as well as divisions. Instead, he commands believers to put on the Lord Jesus as a garment and thus stop thinking about how to gratify the appetites of the sinful nature.

> *Let us behave decently, as in the daytime, not in orgies and drunkenness, not in sexual immorality and debauchery, not in dissension and jealousy. Rather, clothe yourselves with the Lord Jesus Christ, and do not think about how to gratify the desires of the sinful nature.* - Romans 13:13-14

God is pleased when His people offer acceptable sacrifices to Him. They rise to His throne as a sweet-smelling aroma and besides pleasing Him, they cause His holy name to be honoured on earth and in heaven. His status as the eternal King is honoured when man, who He created to glorify Him, offers sacrifices as He has prescribed in His holy word. The prayers of the saints can be truly pleasant to God if they are combined with fasting. The Bible describes the prayers of godly people as a sweet-smelling savour in the eyes of the Lord.

> *And when he had taken it, the four living creatures and the twenty-four elders fell down before the Lamb. Each one had a harp and they were holding golden bowls full of incense, which are the prayers of the saints.* - Revelation 5:8

Fasting is a sacrifice because it entails disciplining the body so that we can make ourselves accessible to God's power and grace. It is laying aside the comforts that the flesh can enjoy so that one may glorify God in their body. The Bible compares this to the manner in which athletes subject themselves to severe training with the intention of winning a reward that has no eternal value. When believers fast, they deal with the hidden intents of the inner man and expose them to the light of God's word so that they can get hold of spiritual realities that are not accessible in any other way. Apostle Paul sees Christian disciplines like fasting as a way of beating the body into shape so that one can lay hold of eternal life that God has promised to all His redeemed.

> *Everyone who competes in the games goes into strict training. They do it to get a crown that will not last; but we do it to get a crown that will last forever. Therefore I do not run like a man running aimlessly; I do not fight like a man beating the air. No, I beat my body and make it my slave so that after I have preached to others, I myself will not be disqualified for the prize. - 1 Corinthians 9:25-27*

Apostle Paul was careful to keep his appetites in check because he knew that there was a possibility of him missing out on eternal life if he allowed his passions to have the better of him. He knew that God's standards of holiness are even stricter for people who have walked with Him closely and those who instruct others (James 3:1). Therefore, he sought to do his duty with commitment and in holiness. Fasting is a great way of beating one's body and its passions and keeping them under control.

Fasting is also a sacrifice because it entails a child

of God willingly submitting to divine discipline. Naturally, sinful humanity enjoys being unruly and wild. However, God wants His children to be disciplined and self-controlled. When they are willing to give up the physical food that nourishes and offers strength to their bodies, God is pleased. Indeed, fasting is a method God has devised for man to willingly subject himself to discipline and divine training so that they may grow in holiness and righteousness. The reward of these virtues is eternal life which cannot be bought with any amount of money.

fasting is a method God has devised for man to willingly subject himself to discipline and divine training so that they may grow in holiness and righteousness

> *Our fathers disciplined us for a little while as they thought best; but God disciplines us for our good, that we may share in his holiness. No discipline seems pleasant at the time, but painful. Later on, however, it produces a harvest of righteousness and peace for those who have been trained by it.* - Hebrews 12:10-11

As believers engage in fasting as a way of sacrificing to God, they should know that God takes sacrifices seriously. As He has shown by the example of Abraham the father of faith, He acts with finality and great significance when His people offer them by faith. Abraham's readiness to offer his only son as a sacrifice touched the heart of God that He made these powerful promises to him.

> *The angel of the LORD called to Abraham from heaven a second time and said, "I swear by myself, declares the LORD, that because you have done this and have not withheld your son, your only son, I will surely bless you and make your descendants as numerous as the stars in the sky and as the sand on the seashore. Your descendants will take possession of the cities of their enemies, and through your offspring all nations on earth will be blessed, because you have obeyed me."* - Genesis 22:15-18

By one act of obedience and sacrifice, Abraham caused a change in all the nations of the world. In the same way, by an act of obedience in fasting per the will of God, believers can witness great changes in the lives of so many people around them because

God honours obedience to His word.

As a sacrifice, fasting is a multifaceted matter. It entails preparing the altar of the heart so that we can glorify God through the praises that emanate from our lips. The words of worship that we utter before God as we are fasting carry great spiritual power and receive divine backing because we speak them from a condition of surrender to His purposes. When we fast, our bodies become vessels that can truly honour God.

> *Through Jesus, therefore, let us continually offer to God a sacrifice of praise - the fruit of lips that confess his name. And do not forget to do good and to share with others, for with such sacrifices God is pleased.* - Hebrews 13:15-16

The Bible also commands us to do good to others as we are fasting by sharing some of our possessions with them. Therefore, we increase the spiritual value of our fasting by willingly sharing some of the things the Lord has given us with those in need. The faith that causes us to fast should also cause us to do works of righteousness.

> *"Is not this the kind of fasting I have chosen: to loose*

the chains of injustice and untie the cords of the yoke, to set the oppressed free and break every yoke? Is it not to share your food with the hungry and to provide the poor wanderer with shelter - when you see the naked, to clothe him, and not to turn away from your own flesh and blood? - Isaiah 58:6-7

As demonstrated by this Scripture, fasting is both an act of obedience and a sacrifice. Faith without works is dead (James 2:17). Therefore, when believers apply the word of God by sharing their possessions to the weak, the poor and the needy as they fast, they increase the spiritual and material value of their fast. These things are very precious in the sight of God as He is looking for worshippers who know His ways so that He can show Himself strong on their behalf.

I will close this chapter by pointing out a warning that is stated in Scripture about sacrifices. The word of God teaches that "obedience is better than sacrifice" (1 Samuel 15:22-23). In simple terms, obedience supersedes sacrifice. Every sacrifice should be done out of obedience to God's word. No amount of fasting can be sufficient to replace obedience to God's word and doing His will.

Chapter 9

FASTING IS PREPARING A SPIRITUAL HIGHWAY

When a Christian engages in fasting, they take up the role of a spiritual builder. The structure they put up is a highway on which the purposes of God for their lives, cities, nations and the whole world can be fulfilled. The Lord has taught me this lesson in a very personal way.

At one point in my life, I took twenty one days of prayer and fasting in which the Holy Spirit ministered to me about preparing a spiritual highway. He taught me that even though one would fast for many days at a time, there are things that God will not do in an instant in their life. Some will take weeks, others will take months and some will take years to be fulfilled. Therefore, the Lord helped me to understand that as one prays, they can move many days into the future and prepare a path for the Lord to work in their life. Like natural highways that require massive groundwork before the final carpeting is done, some things in the lives of children of God need long-term preparation. When done by faith and with understanding, fasting can prove helpful in making a way for the Lord.

God is careful about making plans for the future. In fact, in His word He says that He declares the end from the beginning (Isaiah 46:10). This means that He goes ahead of time to see what the outcome of something will be long before it begins. The birth of Jesus Christ was the most monumental event in the history of mankind. God sent John the Baptist to come as a forerunner of the Messiah and to prepare a highway for Him.

In those days John the Baptist came, preaching in

> *the Desert of Judea and saying, "Repent, for the kingdom of heaven is near." This is he who was spoken of through the prophet Isaiah: "A voice of one calling in the desert, 'Prepare the way for the Lord, make straight paths for him.'"* - Matthew 3:1-3

One of the things John the Baptist did in his ministry was fasting regularly alongside His disciples (Mark 2:18). The assignment he had of making people aware of the Messiah's coming and the work He would do of instituting the kingdom of God on earth was so spiritually significant that it demanded fasting. John's ministry was successful and the Lord approved it by expressing His love for His Son when John baptised Him in the Jordan (Matthew 3:15-17).

Another Bible character that was involved in preparing the highway for the coming of the Son of God was Anna, a prophetess. Her life of continual fasting over many years cleared the path for Jesus to walk in the supernatural assignment the Father had given Him to redeem His people. Despite her age and widowhood, she persisted in the presence of the Lord and lived to witness the birth of the Son of God.

> *There was also a prophetess, Anna, the daughter of Phanuel, of the tribe of Asher. She was very old; she had lived with her husband seven years after her marriage, and then was a widow until she was eighty-four. She never left the temple but worshiped night and day, fasting and praying. Coming up to them at that very moment, she gave thanks to God and spoke about the child to all who were looking forward to the redemption of Jerusalem.* - Luke 2:36-38

Anna's devotion to God in fasting resulted in thanksgiving when what she had committed her life to came into being. Her example demonstrates that one can affect many generations into the future by their dedicated fasting. Spiritual highways that are prepared with fasting will make a more long-lasting impact than those made by prayer without fasting.

Spiritual highways that are prepared with fasting will make a more long-lasting impact than those made by prayer without fasting

The trans-generational impact of fasting has also been exemplified in the Bible by the way the decision of the Ninevites to fast moved the Lord to spare the many children who were in that city. The Lord is a generational God and He desires that current generations make a way for those that will come after them. He identified Himself to Moses as the God of Abraham, Isaac and Jacob (Exodus 3:15). In Jonah's day, He showed His great mercy and compassion for future generations by recognising that there were "more than a hundred and twenty thousand people who cannot tell their right hand from their left" (Jonah 4:11) which refers to children. The fasting of the people of Nineveh to seek God's mercy for their city which He had threatened to destroy made a way for the redemption of a whole generation. The same benefit is available to believers who fast today. They can redeem future generations to God by their fasting.

The word of God also demonstrates that believers can use fasting as a tool of bringing restoration of things that have been ruined over time. One of the benefits of fasting in Isaiah 58 is that God's people shall effect great reestablishment upon the places that have been ransacked by forces of evil and cause great fruitfulness and joy to abound. The Lord promises that those who fast in the way He has prescribed in His word are going to reverse the losses that have resulted from the sins that have been committed over many generations. The foundations of their lives that have been sold out to evil can be divinely restored alongside the walls and streets that have been rendered uninhabitable by the rebellion and sins of many generations.

> *Your people will rebuild the ancient ruins and will raise up the age-old foundations; you will be called Repairer of Broken Walls, Restorer of Streets with Dwellings.* - Isaiah 58:12

Following in the footsteps set in the word of God, believers can repair the damage and restore the losses incurred by their families, cities and nations if they engage the discipline of fasting. The pains, desolation and losses many of them have faced can be reversed when they invoke God's help through dedicated fasting because God takes it very seriously.

Believers can also clear the way for many things that will happen in the future in their lives, families, cities, nations and the world at large by fasting. One thing that all believers need to understand is that life has short-term, long-term and eternal components. It is the will of God that each of His children grows in wisdom so that they can make all the necessary preparation for each of these aspects because they are important. There is need to do well in all so that our lives glorify God. Jesus commanded His disciples to be watchful and prayerful so that they may be found worthy to stand before Him when He returns. He wants His people to be ready when He returns.

> *"Be always on the watch, and pray that you may be able to escape all that is about to happen, and that you may be able to stand before the Son of Man."* - Luke 21:36

This Scripture shows that besides requiring His followers to live circumspectly in this life, Jesus wants them to make preparations for the life to come which is eternal in nature. The prayers believers make for their eternal destinies will be more effective if they are combined with fasting.

It helps to show that one is truly committed to their eternal destiny and they can forego anything to be in right standing with the Lord.

Fasting helps children of God to remove the obstacles on their path of life. The same way engineers use earth movers as they do groundwork when putting up a highway, fasting helps the believer to clear all the debris that the enemy might have placed on their path to hinder them from achieving what God intended. These might include demonic strongholds, self-hatred, poor self-esteem, addictions, curses and the words of evil and jealous men that create roadblocks on the path of God's people. The fullness of life that Jesus came to give His followers (John 10:10) is impossible without fasting.

The same way engineers use earth movers as they do groundwork when putting up a highway, fasting helps the believer to clear all the debris that the enemy might have placed on their path to hinder them from achieving what God intended

Like engineers, believers are builders only that their primary focus is in the spirit realm. Where there is building there is often some work to pull down and uproot the structures that existed previously. This is the commission the Lord gave to Jeremiah when He gave him his prophetic calling (Jeremiah 1:10). Believers share in the same calling because they are priests unto God to declare His marvelous works and establish them upon the earth (1 Peter 2:9). They use their words to pull down and demolish evil structures such as demonic altars and curses. They also use their words as a tool of building up straight paths upon which the Lord can carry out His purposes. Fasting equips believers with the spiritual power and materials they need to transact in the spirit realm to establish the purposes of God. Like God who spoke creation into being from the invisible (Hebrews 11:3), believers receive creative and dynamic power to cause much good to happen when they fast. The wonderful thing about these things they create is that they are eternal because they are spiritual in nature.

The faith-filled confessions, decrees and declarations that believers make as they fast are established in the spirit realm as children of God continue to pursue a right standing with the Lord. The word of God assures His children that they will be able to speak great things into being because they have divine backing. The words spoken by God's people are life and spirit just as those of the Lord (John 6:63). They cause great spiritual and physical transactions to be done in the realm of the spirit.

> *You will also declare a thing, And it will be established for you; So light will shine on your ways. When they cast you down, and you say, 'Exaltation will come!' Then He will save the humble person.* - Job 22:28-29 (NKJV)

Some sins have trans-generational consequences. They include idolatry which God justly punishes by punishing the children for the sins of their fathers to the third and fourth generations. The Bible states this sentence with clarity.

> *"You shall not make for yourself an idol in the form of anything in heaven above or on the earth beneath or in the waters below. You shall not bow down to them or worship them; for I, the LORD your God, am a jealous God, punishing the children for the sin of the fathers to the third and fourth*

generation of those who hate me, but showing love to a thousand generations of those who love me and keep my commandments. - Exodus 20:4-6

When a believer diagnoses that the cause of their problems is generational sin such as idolatry explained in the Scripture above, they can combine their repentance with fasting. As they do that, they plead with God for mercy and in His unfailing compassion and great love, the Lord shall forgive them. He will also gladly restore everything such people have lost because He is predisposed to doing good things for His people. He is gracious and compassionate and wants the best for His children and their offspring. God's mercy is great and it triumphs over judgment (James 2:13).

When believers fast, they take the responsibility of building themselves up in the most holy faith. They are co-workers with Christ and they build on the foundation that Christ has laid (1 Corinthians 3:11). This idea had been practically demonstrated by Nehemiah who took time to pray with fasting when he received a report about the collapse of the wall of Jerusalem (Nehemiah 1:3-4). His fasting caused the Lord to release grace into his life and this activated favour in his life (Nehemiah 2:8). Consequently, the Lord strengthened Nehemiah's hand to do the work He had for him because he took time to fast to prepare a way for the work he needed to do in the spirit realm where all things originate. As a result, the work of rebuilding the wall was done with divine speed because it had God's assistance.

> *So the wall was completed on the twenty-fifth of Elul, in fifty-two days. When all our enemies heard about this, all the surrounding nations were afraid and lost their self-confidence, because they realized that this work had been done with the help of our God.* - Nehemiah 6:15-16

As shown by this example, fasting is a divinely ordained way of preparing a highway for doing in the physical what God wants done in the spiritual. Nehemiah did identification repentance (Nehemiah 1:5-7) and the reproach that had befallen God's people because of the breaking down of the wall of Jerusalem was removed. The same privilege is available for followers of Jesus who will fast.

Believers can achieve great supernatural

results in their physical lives, businesses, careers, ministries and callings if they would fast regularly as they pray for them. Some of the things that hinder progress in the lives of God's people are foundations. The Bible captures this in the form of a rhetorical question.

> *When the foundations are being destroyed, what can the righteous do?* - Psalm 11:3

The best thing to do in such a situation is to seek God and enquire from Him the cause of their failures and non-achievement. The Bible teaches that those who pursue after righteousness should look to the rock from which they are cut as well as the quarry from which they are hewn (Isaiah 55:1). This implies digging deep into one's foundations to deal with every trace of evil that the evil one could use as the foundation of accusation. We can do correctional work into the past and into the future by fasting. The Lord calls on His people to engage in fasting as they deal with such things.

> *'Even now,' declares the LORD, 'return to me with all your heart, with fasting and weeping and mourning.' Rend your heart and not your garments. Return to the LORD your God, for he*

is gracious and compassionate, slow to anger and abounding in love, and he relents from sending calamity. - Joel 2:12-13

If someone is going to obey the command of the Lord by engaging in heartfelt fasting, weeping and mourning for their wayward ways, they are going to activate the promises of God that bring grace, compassion, forgiveness, love and deliverance from destruction.

One thing believers need to understand as they engage in fasting to prepare a spiritual highway is that fasting does not change God. Instead, it changes you. Hagin says, "You're not going to move God. He doesn't move. He's already prone to do certain things, and He's going to do them just as soon as you get in contact with Him and let Him." It is important for us to understand that we cannot twist God's arm to do what He does not want to do.

It is important for us to understand that we cannot twist God's arm to do what He does not want to do

When you seek God wholeheartedly, and that often includes fasting, you get a deeper revelation of Him in His power and majesty. His power to forgive and heal the lives of His people and everything else that concerns them is readily available to those who seek Him with all their hearts with humility, prayer and humbling themselves. He says:

> *If my people, who are called by my name, will humble themselves and pray and seek my face and turn from their wicked ways, then will I hear from heaven and will forgive their sin and will heal their land.* - 2 Chronicles 7:14

God has already given us everything we need for life and godliness in the spirit realm (See 2 Peter 1:3-4 and Ephesians 1:3). However, it behooves us to connect with Him in prayer, His word, fasting and other Christian disciplines so that what is already ours in the unseen world can become ours in the physical. The manifestation of the things God has made available does not come by luck but by the application of spiritual laws and principles by people who have understood them.

Fasting also helps God's servants to prepare ways for spiritual wealth, divine increase and success in ministry. Paul was a zealous Pharisee before His conversion. When he had an encounter with the Lord, he fasted for three days and immediately after that the Lord sent Ananias to lay his hands on him so that he could receive the Holy Spirit (Acts 9:9-12). God's plan for his apostolic ministry that has touched all believers since then especially through the writing of the Bible began unfolding at that point. From then on, Paul's life had a spiritual highway that he could not be moved from.

> ***The manifestation of the things God has made available does not come by luck but by the application of spiritual laws and principles by people who have understood them***

God's system and plan of doing things is progressive. He verified this by promising to give the Israelites land little by little (Exodus 23:30). He needed to give them time to build some spiritual highway in their lives so that when the time came for them to receive the fullness of their inheritance, they would have the spiritual capacity that was necessary to maintain it.

Another way in which fasting prepares a highway is in the area of revival. Writing about the promise of God for the latter rain made in Acts 2:16-18, Prince (1986) avers that fasting is among the keys that God uses in the church of our day to use to implore Him to release the mighty outpouring of the Holy Spirit He has for the last days.

> God has prepared a worldwide outpouring of His Holy Spirit upon His church for these last days. It is God's answer to the desperate needs and pressures of this time. It is His answer for the satanic, ungodly forces that are coming against His people from so many areas, and to the blight and dearth in the church of God. God does not intend to leave His people helpless or at the mercy of all these evil pressures and forces. God has a provision. He has promised to pour out His Spirit and help His people on a supernatural level. However, He requires the condition be met that we seek Him

with prayer and fasting, in a united and collective way.

When revival comes, it brings supernatural productivity, release of those who are in physical and spiritual bondages and stops the flood of the enemy from drowning God's people. The Azusa street revival of the last century is an example of an outpouring that was preceded by many days of prayer and fasting by William J. Seymour, one of the servants of God who were instrumental in that move of God. Liardon (1996) records that Seymour "remained behind the closed doors of his room in prayer and fasting" for many days. This is enough evidence that believers can birth a spiritual awakening in our day through exploiting the power of fasting.

With these examples and illustrations, it is evident that fasting is a powerful tool of preparing a spiritual highway. It has worked in the past and it can work again in our day. It will also work for future generations because God is faithful and always follows His word to perform it.

Chapter 10

DEALING WITH HARD THINGS

As long as we are in this life, we are bound to face difficulties. The Lord has assured us that we are certainly going to encounter hardship as we sojourn towards the heavenly city (John 16:33). However, He has also assured us that He will give us the peace and victory we need if we will let Him. Some of the challenges we face are easy to solve while others are hard. When we face challenges and seemingly impossible situations, it is time to engage the fasting gear.

The Bible gives us several examples of people who fasted when they faced hard things and they overcame them with divine help. God's people might appear as worms in the face of adversities but as they seek Him with fasting, He gives them power to confront and overcome the seemingly impossible.

One example of this is the Prophet Ezra. When the Israelites were returning from captivity, they faced a difficulty because they needed to cross the territories of unfriendly people to get to their homeland. Their enemies could easily have laid ambush for them and captured them (Ezra 8:31). Therefore, they needed divine help because without it they stood no chance of returning to their land safely. Ezra led them to fast.

> *There, by the Ahava Canal, I proclaimed a fast, so that we might humble ourselves before our God and ask him for a safe journey for us and our children, with all our possessions. I was ashamed to ask the king for soldiers and horsemen to protect us from enemies on the road, because we had told the king, "The gracious hand of our God is on everyone who looks to him, but his great anger is against all who*

> *forsake him." So we fasted and petitioned our God about this, and he answered our prayer.* - Ezra 8:21-23

The intention of the people in fasting was to humble themselves before God and pray to Him for a safe journey as well as protection for their offspring and their property. To defend the integrity of their God in the eyes of the people who did not fear Him, Ezra decided to involve the people in a fast to seek God's help. In His faithfulness, the Lord answered their prayer. He does not change and is ready to answer the prayers of His people who are facing hardships today the same way He did in the days of Ezra.

Fasting also offers reinforcement to other spiritual disciplines such as meditating on the word, faith and prayer that help believers to stay grounded in the battlefield of life. It helps followers of Jesus to deal with difficult situations with calmness and power because it gives them assurance that what they decree in the will of God will be established. The Bible declares that God's people shall have their words established because of His divine backing.

> *What you decide on will be done, and light will shine on your ways. When men are brought low and you say, 'Lift them up!' then he will save the downcast.* - Job 22:28-29

From this Scripture, it is evident that when God's people are downcast, those who have sharpened their spiritual senses with fasting can speak a word that will cause their lifting up. God has committed Himself to act on behalf of those who diligently seek Him. He backs up the words of His servants so that He may cause His name to be glorified (Isaiah 44:26a).

Believers need spiritual reinforcement to deal with the hardships that come their way. While it is true that God has given us several spiritual weapons, it is also true some of them require to be used alongside others to be effective. The Bible underscores this fact by stating that a rope of three threads is difficult to break.

> *Though one may be overpowered, two can defend themselves. A cord of three strands is not quickly broken.* - Ecclesiastes 4:12

In other words, the word, prayer and fasting

jointly form a formidable force when it comes to dealing with hardships in life. Believers need to learn and practice this because at one point or other, the situations they face will demand more than one spiritual weapon. Writing about the sevenfold Spirit of God, Isaiah talks about the Spirit of might (Isaiah 11:2). This aspect of the Spirit of God helps us to have divine reinforcement in times of difficulty. Might is power that overcomes opposition. God has made provision for His people to seek Him so that they can activate His mighty power in their lives.

the word, prayer and fasting jointly form a formidable force when it comes to dealing with hardships in life. Believers need to learn and practice this because at one point or other, the situations they face will demand more than one spiritual weapon

The Lord Jesus demonstrated that He knew His followers would have to face difficult things. He used the metaphor of mountains to refer to those challenges. He told His disciples that they would have the power to command mountains to move if they would take time to develop their faith.

> *"I tell you the truth, if anyone says to this mountain, 'Go, throw yourself into the sea,' and does not doubt in his heart but believes that what he says will happen, it will be done for him."* - Mark 11:23

This example shows the efficiency and power of faith in making the impossible happen. While we may not face literal mountains that we need to have removed from our way, we will certainly need the power of God to help us overcome big challenges that will no doubt come our way in life. This is meant to be the life of a man or woman of faith. Jesus showed this when He cursed an unfruitful fig tree and it withered with immediate effect.

> *Seeing a fig tree by the road, he went up to it but found nothing on it except leaves. Then he said to it, "May you never bear fruit again!" Immediately the tree withered.* - Matthew 21:19

This was a supernatural occurrence that was not easy to accomplish for an ordinary human being. The disciples were amazed that His words carried so much power. He responded to them that He was able to do that because of His faith in God.

This kind of faith comes from believing the Word and reinforcing it with fasting. By virtue of His fast, Jesus had the spiritual capital necessary to cause great things to happen. He has commanded His followers to build up their faith so that they can walk in supernatural manifestations just like He did.

> *He replied, "If you have faith as small as a mustard seed, you can say to this mulberry tree, 'Be uprooted and planted in the sea,' and it will obey you.* - Luke 17:6

The Lord has also taught His followers that working powerful miracles is within their reach if they follow His footsteps.

> *Jesus replied, "I tell you the truth, if you have faith and do not doubt, not only can you do what was done to the fig tree, but also you can say to this mountain, 'Go, throw yourself into the sea,' and it will be done.* - Matthew 21:21

Jesus' ability to do the extraordinary by the words of His mouth was not a matter of luck. Those things did not just happen because He was the Son of God. Rather, He did the impossible with ease because His ministry was Spirit-led and

He had taken time to seek the God who turns impossibilities into possibilities. He fasted forty days and forty nights at the beginning of His ministry.

Consider His ministry of driving out evil spirits from people. Casting out demons is not an easy task that can be done by just anybody. However, Jesus did it with ease because of His history of seeking God with fasting for a considerable time. He was consequently empowered by the Spirit of God to cast out demons and heal the sick with a word.

> *When evening came, many who were demon-possessed were brought to him, and he drove out the spirits with a word and healed all the sick.* - Matthew 8:16

This shows that when a person has supernatural backing, the otherwise impossible becomes a possibility. Fasting is one of the most effective ways of appropriating God's power into one's life. The people of Jesus' day observed His ministry and were astounded that He had unusual divine authority and that even evil spirits (that have some measure of power and potential to cause much evil and harm) obeyed Him without question.

> *The people were all so amazed that they asked each other, "What is this? A new teaching - and with authority! He even gives orders to evil spirits and they obey him."* - Mark 1:27

Jesus has promised that His followers will do even greater things than the ones He did (John 14:12). However, such astonishing manifestations of the glory and power of God are only possible with serious commitment to Him and with prayer and fasting.

The Lord has a great assignment for His followers today. This includes setting the oppressed free, releasing those that are bound in poverty, addictions, generational bondages and curses. His word says the kind of fasting He has chosen entails losing the chains of injustice as well as untying the cords of satanic yokes and setting those who have been plagued free.

> *"Is not this the kind of fasting I have chosen: to loose the chains of injustice and untie the cords of the yoke, to set the oppressed free and break every yoke?* - Isaiah 58:6

Yokes are not easy. They are demonically enforced bondages that enslave and bind people. They operate alongside the strongholds of the enemy to keep people under what the Lord wants lifted and free. The spiritual weapons that the Lord gives to His people are meant to be powerful enough to dethrone those strongholds and enthrone the Lord in the lives of His people. That way, the mountains of life are leveled and challenges are overcome and thus God is glorified.

As a person fasts, they gain spiritual strength so that their words become like the words of God. They receive creative power that can work extraordinary miracles that are not possible for people who do not fast. They become like fire and hammer that can be used to destroy and burn down evils and hardships (Jeremiah 23:29). Jesus has taught us

As a person fasts, they gain spiritual strength so that their words become like the words of God. They receive creative power that can work extraordinary miracles that are not possible for people who do not fast

that there are certain categories of evil spirits that will not go out without prayer and fasting.

> *"However, this kind does not go out except by prayer and fasting."* - Matthew 17:21 (NKJV)

That means that no matter how one may be determined to get rid of these spirits and the experience they might have in driving away evil powers, this category of spirits will not leave if they have not prayed and fasted. This is why it is so important for workers in the body of Christ to practice regular fasting so that they can build their spiritual capacity to minister to those in need. Stubborn demons need great spiritual power to evict them from people.

Jesus had to fast to execute His liberation and deliverance mandate which was without a doubt a demanding assignment. It was not easy for Him to bear the cross and die in our place although He was sinless. At one point when He was praying, He asked the Father to remove the imminent cup of suffering from Him because He knew it would not be easy (Luke 22:42). Although His redemptive work had been foretold by many prophets and it was the perfect will of God for Him, He had to fast to actualise it. At the end of His fast, He made what one might describe as His inauguration address and He detailed the hard things His ministry had come to confront and overcome.

> *"The Spirit of the Lord is on me, because he has anointed me to preach good news to the poor. He has sent me to proclaim freedom for the prisoners and recovery of sight for the blind, to release the oppressed, to proclaim the year of the Lord's favor.*
> - Luke 4:18-19

Jesus had prisoners to set free and many blind people whose sight He was to restore. These are not easy things and He needed divine power to do them. The fact that He made this proclamation at the end of His forty days fast is significant because He needed to have gone through fasting to be equipped for His assignment.

Believers need to learn some lessons from the natural world and apply them in their fasting to be able to deal with hard things. The same way businesspeople do not go abroad to get commodities that are readily available locally, believers need to engage a higher spiritual gear as they engage in fasting. They thus need to seek spiritual empowerment to face difficulties when they engage in fasting. In other words, it is not enough to fast without asking God to fill you with His power to enable you to do the extraordinary. Some of these extraordinary things include restoring what the enemy has stolen from the lives of individuals, families, cities and nations (see Isaiah 58:12).

Through fasting, one receives spiritual muscles to deal with hard yokes and situations. The yoke is symbolic of boundaries and slavery. They are part of the many tools Satan uses to oppress and limit God's people. The word of God promises that the activity of the Holy Spirit, whose physical symbol is the anointing oil, will destroy the yokes of the devil.

> *It shall come to pass in that day That his burden will be taken away from your shoulder, And his yoke from your neck, And the yoke will be destroyed because of the anointing oil.* - Isaiah 10:27 (NKJV)

Believers are engaged in a spiritual warfare

against forces of evil (Ephesians 6:12). These powers are grouped in ranks. The higher in hierarchy the spiritual force one is pitted against, the stronger the power and force a believer will need to apply to dethrone them. Some of them like principalities have considerable power. That is why Jesus commanded His disciples to wage warfare with wisdom by first biding the strongman before taking his spoil (Matthew 12:29).

Some of the hard things people face are personal while others have to do with families, tribes, cities or nations. To surmount them, believers need to engage in fasting so that they can receive spiritual backing to break free from them. For instance, some countries especially in Africa have faced problems with chronic tribalism, rampant corruption and widespread idolatry. To successfully deal with such problems and uproot them, God's people will need to fast as they approach Him for a lasting solution. He invites them to seek Him with humility.

> *"Come now, let us reason together," says the LORD. "Though your sins are like scarlet, they shall be as white as snow; though they are red as crimson, they shall be like wool."* - Isaiah 1:18

The same is true of personal sins that are deep-rooted and repetitive. Many people have lived in deep spiritual dungeons because of yokes of iniquity and secret sins. The Psalmist recognised this and pleaded with the Lord not to allow secret sins to master him (Psalm 19:12-13). Some secret sins have very deep roots and they hinder God's people from manifesting their greatness because they act as chains to limit their movement and freedom. When such captives engage in fasting and reinforce it with serious prayers and deep meditation of the word of God, those problems cave in and fade into insignificance.

Fasting helps God's people to deal with desperate conditions. Situations that one would consider irreversible can be reversed by the power of prayer and fasting. Dead things can be brought back to life by prayer and fasting because it avails the supernatural power that is at God's disposal. The Lord says that nothing is too hard for Him and thus when His people seek Him with diligence, He can release some of His limitless power into their lives to help them deal with hard things.

I am the LORD, the God of all mankind. Is anything too hard for me? - Jeremiah 32:27

One of the most outstanding examples of a person who faced a difficult life is Jabez. The Bible records that he was born in excruciating pain and as a result, his mother had given him that name which means pain. This is the account of his life.

Jabez was more honorable than his brothers. His mother had named him Jabez, saying, "I gave birth to him in pain." Jabez cried out to the God of Israel, "Oh, that you would bless me and enlarge my territory! Let your hand be with me, and keep me from harm so that I will be free from pain." And God granted his request. -1 Chronicles 4:9-10

The difficulty that Jabez faced was severe and his prayer was not necessarily as simple as it is recorded in Scripture. It was a journey he took to seek God. He cried to the Lord which means that he made a desperate cry. It is also possible that he reinforced his prayer with fasting. While we may not know how many days he took in seeking God, we are sure that the kind of result he got is not obtained easily. His breakthrough was not instant because his problem had been running for a long time from when he was born. The same kind of help and deliverance is available to those who will seek God because of the bondages they might be in. God has not changed and He is eager to do good to His people.

Some of the more difficult problems we face might require several periods of fasting. It is the will of the Lord that His people learn to count the cost and pay the price for the people they desire to become (Luke 14:28-33). God rewards those who diligently seek Him (Hebrews 11:6). If we seek Him diligently, He will repay us handsomely. He is a God who keeps His covenant to those who seek Him.

It is true that prayer changes things. But of all prayers, the fasting prayer has the greatest effect of all. Yes, it is the master key to making the impossible possible

There is great power to overcome hardships for those who know the secret of fasting. Lindsay (1974) observes that when all else fails, fasting and prayer can turn the tide. He adds, "It is true that prayer changes things. But of all prayers, the fasting prayer has the greatest effect of all. Yes, it is the master key to making the impossible possible."

Every believer needs to know that they should not give up on seeking the face of God with fasting. Some of the hard things that we are fighting against might take some time and require considerable effort. However, when one is consistent and determined, they will eventually emerge victorious. Persistence wears out resistance.

> *"'If you can'?" said Jesus. "Everything is possible for him who believes."* - Mark 9:23

The Lord has given us the key of overcoming all hardships. The only thing that remains is us to take up the call and run with it.

Conclusion

There is atomic power in fasting especially if it is done according to the word of God. If we could exploit it, we would change our lives and those of other people forever. It is therefore unfortunate that not enough people practice this discipline with commitment and with understanding.

We should all appreciate the fact that God will not come into our lives without our invitation. By fasting, we can ask Him to open doors in our lives that no man can close. This can happen if we will offer constant prayers for our lives, ministries, careers, calling and children. All followers of Jesus also need to know that the greatest work on earth is the work of prayer and that it cannot be separated from fasting.

The lessons in the word of God on fasting are clear. None of us should wait for a special sign from heaven to begin a lifestyle of regular fasting. Believers just need to make a decision to act on the word of God in obedience and begin to seek God with fasting. One of the most influential servants of God of the last century, Kenneth Hagin records that when he first went out in the field ministry, he set aside two days every week – Tuesday and Thursdays and devoted them to prayer and fasting. He admits that he "wasn't led of the Lord to do it," but just fasted two days a week. He also says that he took the time he would have spent eating to pray. That is what many believers who have been dormant in this area need to do without any delay.

Sadly, many people make the mistake of waiting to hear a special message or revelation from God so that they can engage in fasting. Such people end up not fasting. We should not wait for God to speak on a matter He has made so clear in His word. Hagin additionally advises that "fasting will not do you much good if you're not going to spend extra time praying, waiting on God." He testifies that he "made the greatest spiritual strides yet in my ministry" during the time he used to fast two days a week. He would simply shut himself up in his church and spend many hours praying. This is exactly what many Christians need to do today.

We are not waiting on God; He is waiting on us to rise and shine for our light has come. The sooner we realise this, the better for our lives, ministries, families and nations are going to be. Fasting is the link that is missing in the lives of so many people. This is especially important for people who truly desire to glorify God through their lives and for those who are in ministry and desire to show the world the splendour of God. Brooks (2012) observes:

> The reason the church does not see greater manifestations of God's power is because of a failure to fast and pray. If you want to have true power with God and see miracles like we see in the Bible which the great saints of old experienced, then we must also take up the mantle of fasting and prayer. The desperate needs of our end-time generation cannot be met any other way. The faith that moves mountains, raises the dead, opens blind eyes, heals the sick, and obtains results that are otherwise out of reach are found through the release of God's nuclear

power—fasting and prayer.

God rewards diligent seekers and is not a respecter of persons (Acts 10:34). He avails His great power and grace to those who humble themselves before Him. If we will rely on the guidance of the Holy Spirit to help us know God better, we will be equipped to work exploits in our generation.

It is my sincere hope and prayer that after reading this book and understanding the many benefits you can derive from fasting, you will commit yourself to a consistent lifestyle of fasting. I can tell you without fear of contradiction that fasting activates supernatural power and you can be a partaker of this divine power if you will take the necessary steps.

May the grace of fasting rest upon your life from now henceforth in the mighty name of Jesus Christ! Shalom!

REFERENCES

Brooks, S. (2012). *Fasting and Prayer: God's Nuclear Power.* Pennsylvania: Destiny Image

Franklin, J. (2008). *Fasting.* Lake Mary, FL: Charisma House

Hagin, K. (1981). *A Commonsense Guide to Fasting.* Tulsa, OK: Kenneth Hagin Ministries

Liardon, R. (1996). *God's Generals: Why They Succeeded and Why Some Failed.* Kensington, PA: Whitaker House

Lindsay, G. (1974). *Prayer and Fasting: The Master Key to the Impossible.* Dallas, TX: Christ for the Nations Inc.

Ormatian, S. (1999). *Greater Health God's Way: Seven Steps to Inner and Outer Beauty.* Oregon: Harvest House Publishers.

Prince, D. (1973). *Shaping History through Prayer and Fasting.* New Kensington, PA: Whitaker House

Prince, D. (1986). *Fasting.* New Kensington: Whitaker House

Wallis, A. (1968). *God's Chosen Fast.* Pennsylvania: Christian Literature Crusade

Other Books by Apostle John K. William

1. Spiritual Maturity
2. Ten Principles of Success in Ministry
3. Manifesting Your Glory
4. Dealing with Foundations and Altars
5. Ingredients of Success
6. Battles of Life
7. Choosing the Marriage Partner
8. Serving God
9. Making Impact Through the Power of Prayer
10. Spiritual Hedge
11. Spiritual Race
12. The Treasure of the Gospel
13. Great Questions of Destiny
14. The Weight of the Matter
15. The power of Acceptable Sacrifice
16. Can God Trust You?
17. The Beauty of a Transformed Life
18. Pursuing Your Destiny
19. God's Scoring Board
20. Sin as Cancer
21. Pillars of Walking with God

22. Wealth without Wings
23. Setting Your Standard
24. Provoked to Greatness
25. Uzito wa Jambo (Swahili version of *The Weight of a Matter*)
26. Spiritual Diagnosis
27. Commitment as a key to success
28. The Life of an Eagle
29. Priorities in Life
30. Becoming a Spiritual Builder
31. Spiritual Capital for your Destiny

For Inquiries or to order these books and other materials, contact us through: +254 715 940 000

Kindly give us your feedback about this book by writing to:

apostlekimanifeedback@gmail.com

www.ingramcontent.com/pod-product-compliance
Lightning Source LLC
LaVergne TN
LVHW010550160826
845677LV00013B/3072
* 9 7 8 9 9 6 6 8 2 1 9 5 9 *